A Step toward Democracy

The December 1989 Elections in Taiwan, Republic of China

Martin L. Lasater

The AEI Press

Publisher for the American Enterprise Institute

WASHINGTON, D. C.

Martin L. Lasater is president of the Pacific Council.

Distributed by arrangement with

University Press of America, Inc.
4720 Boston Way   3 Henrietta Street
Lanham, Md. 20706   London WC2E 8LU England

1 3 5 7 9 10 8 6 4 2

AEI Special Analyses 90-3

Printed in the United States of America

Contents

LIST OF TABLES

Foreword

The American Enterprise Institute has, over the course of a quarter-century, conducted more than a dozen election studies in all corners of the globe, building up a repertoire of experience and a reputation for solid observation and analysis of high quality and reliability. At the same time, the institute is pleased to have maintained a close association with the Republic of China on Taiwan and with the Institute of International Relations in Taipei. It was thus with particular enthusiasm that AEI responded in July 1989 to a request by Shaw Yu-ming, the director-general of the Government Information Office in Taipei, to conduct an election watch of the Republic of China's first widely contested democratic election to be held in December of that year.

An election watch team was thereby assembled under the leadership of Howard Penniman, who has led many such teams in the past and who has written several of AEI's studies in this field. Dr. Penniman is, in fact, perhaps America's leading expert on the electoral transition to democracy. The team consisted of a number of persons intimately familiar either with this field or with Taiwan, or both. Martin Lasater was chosen to write the study of the December election outcome as well as a background analysis and a creative essay on what the elections mean for Taiwan's domestic and international future. One of America's leading students of Taiwan, Dr. Lasater has observed the political scene there for many years. Other members of the team were Raymond Gastil, former editor of *Freedom Survey*, James A. Robinson, president emeritus of the University of West Florida, and Richard Smolka of American University. All three have had extensive election watch experience internationally and have also been close observers of the Taiwan political scene.

Members of the team other than Dr. Lasater were encouraged to write supplementary statements on specific areas of personal interest. The statements of Raymond Gastil and James Robinson are included at the end of the study as appendixes B and C. Their comments are not intended as minority reports but rather are offered as additional perspectives on the continuing evolution of democracy on Taiwan.

The team assembled in Taipei on November 27, 1989, and remained until December 4. James Robinson arrived in Taipei a week earlier to conduct personal interviews, and Martin Lasater remained in Taiwan the week following the elections for follow-up interviews. The AEI team became part of a larger group of U.S. scholars who followed an extensive program organized by the Republic of China (ROC) Ministry of Foreign Affairs and Government Information Office. Members of the delegation were free to travel where they pleased and to interview whomever they chose. Although each team member took advantage of this opportunity, the majority of the delegation's time during the period of November 27–December 2 was spent according to the schedule.

November 27
- call on Shaw Yu-ming, director-general of the Government Information Office
- call on Antonio Chiang, publisher of the *New Journalists Magazine*
- call on You Ching, candidate for Taipei County magistrate

November 28
- briefing at headquarters of the Kuomintang
- briefing at the Central Election Commission
- briefing at headquarters of the Democratic Progressive party

November 29 (AEI splits into two teams for November 29–30, one going to Taichung and Hsinchu and the other traveling to Kaohsiung.)

Taichung-Hsinchu group
- briefing at Taichung City chapter of Kuomintang
- call on Hong Chao-nan, candidate for Legislative Yuan
- call on Lin Poh-jung, candidate for Taichung City mayor
- visit public-sponsored campaign forum

Kaohsiung group
- briefing at Kaohsiung County chapter of Kuomintang
- call on Chen Yih-chiu, candidate for Kaohsiung County magistrate
- visit campaign forum

November 30
Taichung-Hsinchu group
- call on Shen Chih-huei, candidate for Legislative Yuan
- call on Hsu Jong-su, candidate for Taichung City mayor

- call on Ton Shen-nan, candidate for Hsinchu City mayor
- call on Shih Chi-mei, candidate for Hsinchu City mayor

Kaohsiung group
- call on Wang Chin-ping, candidate for Legislative Yuan
- call on Yu Cheng-hsien, candidate for Legislative Yuan
- call on Yu Chen Yueh-ying, candidate for Kaohsiung County magistrate
- call on Huang Ho-chin, candidate for Legislative Yuan

December 1
- briefing by Taipei City Election Commission
- visit campaign forum

December 2 (election day)
- visit polling stations
- visit local vote-counting stations
- visit Taipei City Vote-Counting Center
- visit the Central Vote-Counting Center

December 3
- with other American scholars' delegations present findings to American Institute in Taiwan and U.S. congressional delegation led by Congressman Stephen J. Solarz, chairman, House Subcommittee on Asian and Pacific Affairs, Committee on Foreign Affairs
- assemble to discuss contents of final report

December 4
- depart for the United States. Martin Lasater remains for a further week of interviews and analysis of local media reports on the elections.

The following report reflects the AEI election observer team's consensus on the step toward democracy that the December 2, 1989, elections on Taiwan represent. The report stresses the *process* of democracy on Taiwan and, hence, considers the 1989 elections in the broader context of political development on Taiwan over the past decade. Further, to distinguish this report from the several others that were produced by American observer teams, the 1989 election results are analyzed for their possible impact on U.S. interests and policy, particularly as these relate to the Taiwan issue as an important component of Sino-American relations.

Thomas W. Robinson
Director, China Studies Program
American Enterprise Institute

1
Introduction

On December 2, 1989, the Republic of China (ROC) on Taiwan held elections for 293 seats in the national, provincial, and local government. Of the 293 seats, 101 were for the Legislative Yuan (or parliament of the nation), 77 for the Provincial Assembly of Taiwan, 51 for the Taipei City Council, 43 for the Kaohsiung City Council, 16 for county magistrate seats, and 5 for mayoral seats.

Altogether, 722 candidates competed for these seats, including 302 candidates for the Legislative Yuan, 157 candidates for the Taiwan Provincial Assembly, 100 for the Taipei City Council, 94 for the Kaohsiung City Council, and 69 for the mayoral and magistrate seats (see table 1–1).

TABLE 1–1
NUMBER OF CONTESTED SEATS AND CANDIDATES FOR THE
1989 ELECTIONS IN THE REPUBLIC OF CHINA

Elected Body	Seats	Candidates
Legislative Yuan	101	302
Taiwan Provincial Assembly	77	157
Taipei City Council	51	100
Kaohsiung City Council	43	94
Mayors and magistrates	21	69
Total	293	722

The elections were considered an important test for democracy on Taiwan, because for the first time since the Nationalist government withdrew to Taiwan following its 1949 defeat on mainland China at the hands of the Chinese Communists, the ruling Nationalist party, or Kuomintang

(KMT), competed in free elections with other major political parties for the right to govern.

The elections were significant for other reasons as well: the elections were the first since martial law was lifted in June 1987, and they were the first since the legalization of new political parties in February 1989. For the first time, a majority of the candidates were selected through party primaries. The number of seats contested was also the largest since the 1947 elections on mainland China, giving voters an exceptional opportunity to demonstrate their preferences on key national and local issues.

The elections were hotly contested by the largest number of candidates ever to enter an election on Taiwan (see table 1–2). The majority KMT fielded a total of 346 candidates, or 48 percent of the 722 individuals competing in the elections. The principal opposition, the Democratic Progressive party (DPP), sent 163 candidates into the elections. DPP candidates were thus about 22 percent of the total.

The China Democratic Socialist party and the Young China party (both of which moved to Taiwan with the Nationalists in 1949) registered 5 and 4 candidates, respectively. Two newly formed parties, the Labor party and the Worker's party, had 15 and 4 candidates in the elections. Other parties had a total of 14 candidates. Independents, many of whom were KMT or DPP running against the parties' wishes, totaled 171, or 24 percent of the candidates.

TABLE 1–2

THE PARTY AFFILIATION OF CANDIDATES RUNNING IN THE
1989 ELECTIONS IN THE REPUBLIC OF CHINA

Affiliation	Number of Candidates	Percentage of Total
KMT	346	47.9
DPP	163	22.5
Labor party	15	2.1
Democratic Socialist party	5	0.7
Young China party	4	0.5
Worker's party	4	0.5
Other parties	14	1.9
Independents	171	23.7
Total candidates	722	99.8

NOTE: Percentages do not add to 100 because of rounding.

TABLE 1–3
LEGISLATIVE ELECTION RESULTS, 1989
(number of seats and percentage of vote won)

Office	Kuomintang		Democratic Pro-gressive Party		Labor Party		Other	
	Number	%	Number	%	Number	%	Number	%
Legislative Yuan	72	71.3	21	20.8	0	0	8	7.9
Provincial Assembly	54	70.1	16	20.8	0	0	7	9.1
Taipei City Council	36	70.6	14	27.5	0	0	1	2.0
Kaohsiung City Council	29	67.4	8	18.6	1	2.3	5	11.6
Local a	14	66.7	6	28.6	0	0	1	4.8
Totals	205	70.0	65	22.2	1	0.3	22	7.5

NOTE: Percentages do not add to 100 because of rounding.
a. County magistrates and city mayors.

The December 1989 elections were held with very few serious incidents and under conditions most observers thought more free and fair than previous elections on Taiwan. Voter turnout was over 75 percent of registered voters.

Of the 101 available Legislative Yuan seats, the KMT won 72 seats (71 percent), the DPP won 21 seats (21 percent), and others won 8 seats (8 percent) (see table 1–3). In the race for the 77 Provincial Assembly seats, the KMT won 54 seats (70 percent), the DPP captured 16 seats (21 percent), and others won 7 seats (9 percent). Of the 51 Taipei City Council seats up for election, the KMT won 36 seats (71 percent), the DPP won 14 seats (27 percent), and others won 1 seat (2 percent).

Seats available for the Kaohsiung City Council totaled 43. Of these, the KMT won 29 seats (67 percent), the DPP won 8 seats (19 percent), the Labor party won 1 seat (2 percent), and others won 5 seats (12 percent). Out of the 21 county magistrate and city mayor seats, the KMT won 14 seats (67 percent), the DPP won 6 seats (29 percent), and others won 1 seat (5 percent).

The KMT won about 70 percent of the total seats and about 60 percent of the vote, while the DPP won about 22 percent of available seats and 31 percent of the votes. Other parties and independent candidates won about 8 percent of the seats and votes. As for the number of winning candidates in relation to the number of total candidates fielded by the party, the KMT had a 59.2 percent success rate; the DPP had a 39.9 percent rate; the Labor party a 6.7 percent rate; the Young China party, China Democratic Socialist party, and Worker's party a 0 percent success rate; and other parties and independents an 11.9 percent success rate.

The significance of the results of the December 1989 elections can be understood only within the context of the development of democracy on Taiwan. The first part of this volume will discuss the background of the elections as it bears on the political evolution on Taiwan since 1949. The next part discusses the results of the December 1989 elections. The last part analyzes these results and speculates on what they might mean for the future of Taiwan and the interests of the United States. Appendix A presents the results of various elections from 1951 to 1986. Appendix B, contributed by Raymond D. Gastil, evaluates the 1989 elections, while appendix C, by James A. Robinson, discusses Taiwan's developing political institutions.

2
Background to the Elections

In contrast to the economic "miracle" of Taiwan, the evolution of Taiwan's political system has been much slower. From 1949 until very recently, Taiwan was under a system of martial law that tightly controlled political activity on the island.

Beginning in 1986, however, the pace of Taiwan's political development increased rapidly. In the space of three years, the government lifted martial law, allowed the formation of new political parties, lifted restrictions on the press, removed bans on street demonstrations, elected as president of the Republic of China and chairman of the Kuomintang a native-born Taiwanese, held free elections in a multiparty environment, and began pensioning off senior parliamentarians who had held office without reelection since 1947.

The process of political liberalization continues; but in a remarkably brief time, Taiwan has moved in a significant way from an authoritarian regime dominated by the KMT toward a multiparty democracy in which the KMT still dominates but increasingly must compete for power with other political parties.

The Kuomintang, or Nationalist Party

The rapidity with which political reforms were implemented on Taiwan after 1986 caught most Western observers by surprise, although KMT goals and objectives have always included a commitment to the eventual establishment of democracy.

The KMT originated from various revolutionary parties dedicated to the overthrow of the Manchu, or Qing, dynasty in October 1911. Its present name was adopted in 1924, when Sun Yat-sen, founder of the Republic of China, reorganized the KMT along Leninist lines. Sun formed the KMT to achieve his Three Principles of the People: national

5

independence, political democracy, and social well-being.

The Three Principles of the People represent the KMT's ideological goals. According to Sun, "nationalism" means an equal and independent status for China in the world, an equal status for all ethnic groups in China, and the restoration and renaissance of traditional Chinese culture. "Democracy" is intended to ensure that all Chinese people have civil liberties, including political power. "Social well-being," or people's livelihood, implies a welfare state with a prosperous economy and a just society. This third principle advocates a free enterprise economic system with elements of government planning so that national wealth can be rapidly accumulated and equitably distributed.

Under Sun's direction, the ROC government was organized into five branches, or *yuan*. Three were adopted from western political traditions: the Executive Yuan, the Legislative Yuan, and the Judicial Yuan. Two were adopted from traditional Chinese political systems: an Examination Yuan to select members of the civil service and a Control Yuan to enforce standards of behavior among government officials. A National Assembly elected by the people was responsible for approving the Constitution and amendments and for electing the president of the ROC.

In the Republic of China, legislative responsibilities are shared by the Legislative Yuan, whose members serve three-year terms and who are directly elected; the Control Yuan, whose members serve six-year terms and who are indirectly elected; and the National Assembly, whose members also serve six-year terms but who are directly elected. As will be explained shortly, most of the officials currently holding these offices were elected only once—on mainland China in 1947.

As the ruling party, the KMT conducts its relations with the government by implementing policies through the work of party members in the government. Political cadres in the government include appointed ministers and vice-ministers in the Executive Yuan and elected representatives in the National Assembly, Legislative Yuan, Control Yuan, and the provincial, municipal, county, township, and village assemblies and councils. The KMT selects the individuals for these posts and, if necessary, trains them for government appointment. The KMT assists its nominated candidates in running for office as well.

At present, the KMT has about 2.5 million members out of a total population on Taiwan of 20 million. The KMT's supreme organ is the National Congress, which convenes every four years or so. The last party congress, the thirteenth, was held in July 1988. When the Congress is not in session, the KMT is governed by the Central Committee, which meets every year in plenary sessions. Day-to-day activities are overseen

6

by the Central Standing Committee, which meets weekly. The Central Standing Committee is headed by a chairman who is usually the president of the ROC as well. He is assisted by a group of party counselors, the secretary general of the party, and three deputy secretary generals. Below the central level are congresses for provinces, counties and cities, and districts.

The History of the KMT. Sun theorized that the ROC would go through three stages of development to implement the Three Principles of the People. The first would be military administration to unite the country, the second would be political tutelage under the KMT to educate the Chinese people in exercising their political rights, and the third and final stage would be constitutional democracy.

In fact, depending upon which stage of history one is examining, KMT rule can be characterized as a revolutionary regime, a military dictatorship, an authoritarian regime, or an evolving democracy. During the early 1920s, for example, the KMT was organized along Leninist revolutionary lines with the help of Comintern agents. During the period 1927 to 1947, General Chiang Kai-shek, who took over the leadership of the KMT following Sun's death in 1925, ruled the ROC as a military dictator in constant warfare against the warlords, Communists, and Japanese.

Elections were held in those areas of China under Nationalist control in 1947, and a constitution guaranteeing civil liberties was adopted. Shortly thereafter, however, martial law was declared because of deteriorating conditions brought about by the civil war fought between the KMT and the Communists. From 1948 (and especially since 1949, when the ROC was reduced to the province of Taiwan) until 1987, the ROC was under martial law provisions of the Temporary Provisions Effective during the Period of Communist Rebellion. Although martial law gave the ROC's president extraordinary power to prosecute the war against the Communists, it denied the ROC citizens on Taiwan many of the basic rights defined in the 1947 Constitution.

Martial law was formally abolished by the ROC in July 1987, although a National Security Law was subsequently passed that retained for the government strong powers to counter perceived threats of sedition. Since the lifting of martial law, the KMT has steadily moved Taiwan toward constitutional democracy.[1] From February through December 1989, over forty political parties, aside from the KMT, registered to become legal on Taiwan. The KMT and fifteen other political parties openly competed for seats in the December 1989 elections.

Several major events in KMT history have had a profound impact on

7

Taiwan's domestic political development. When the Nationalists first arrived in Taiwan in 1945 after fifty years of Japanese rule,[2] many soldiers treated the Taiwanese as collaborators with the Japanese.[3] Atrocities occurred, culminating in the riots of early 1947 in which several thousand Taiwanese were killed.[4] Tensions between the Taiwanese and the mainlanders remained high for decades, resulting in political, economic, and social divisions that remain on the island today. Despite the gradual weakening of these divisions through intermarriage and a common educational system, continued Taiwanese antagonism toward the mainlanders is one important element in modern political opposition to the KMT.

Another key development in KMT history occurred in 1950, the year after the Nationalists retreated to Taiwan from the mainland. Aware that many of its policies had contributed to the loss of mainland China and that its early occupation of Taiwan had been seriously misdirected, the KMT undertook a comprehensive self-examination and reformation.

In one decision with far-reaching consequences, the KMT determined that, instead of using military means alone to defeat the Communists, it would use political and economic means to undermine Beijing and regain the support of the Chinese people. Under this strategy, Taiwan was to become a model province of the Three Principles of the People in the expectation that the Communist regime on the mainland would eventually collapse.

Once this strategy was adopted, policy priorities of the KMT shifted from strict military confrontation with the People's Republic of China (PRC) to the economic, social, and political development of Taiwan. This meant raising the standard of living of the people of Taiwan, improving the quality of their life, and gradually implementing the democracy called for by Sun Yat-sen.

The decision to make Taiwan a model province permitted a tacit understanding to be reached between the mainlanders (roughly 15 percent of Taiwan's population) and the Taiwanese (85 percent of the population): the mainlanders would dominate national politics, while Taiwanese (mostly members of the KMT but some independents) could dominate local and provincial politics. This tacit understanding, coupled with the island's rapid economic growth, led to the retention of political control of Taiwan by the mainlanders, and the exercise of economic power by the Taiwanese.

This arrangement helped lessen hostility between the two social groups and worked reasonably well for several decades. The few Taiwanese who openly criticized fundamental KMT policies were dealt with harshly under martial law, usually being jailed for lengthy sentences or, in some cases, killed.[5] A number of Taiwanese political activists fled Taiwan to take up anti-KMT causes in Japan and the United States. Many of these dissidents advocated that Taiwan should become an independent nation, free from either KMT or Communist mainlander control.

Political Liberalization

Another major change in KMT policy began in the late 1970s, when a series of external and internal pressures caused the Nationalists to begin liberalization of Taiwan's political system. These pressures included:

- the increased diplomatic isolation of the ROC
- the corresponding rise in prestige and influence of the rival regime in Beijing
- the shift in U.S. diplomatic recognition from the ROC to the PRC
- the rise of Taiwan's middle class and a well-educated public, both of which demanded more political freedom
- the perception of a reduced PRC military threat to Taiwan
- the increasingly antiquated ROC parliament, obviously in need of reform
- the more open attitude toward the discussion of sensitive political issues on Taiwan
- the rise in power of reform-minded KMT leaders, who suggested that the political system needed to be liberalized
- the mounting criticism of martial law and human rights violations from foreigners, especially Americans
- the growing consensus within Taiwan that martial law had fulfilled its purpose of stabilizing the island and that its continuation would be harmful to the interests of the ROC and Taiwan

Two of the most significant political reforms initiated in the late 1970s were steps toward the "Taiwanization" of the KMT and the ROC government and the recruitment of Western-trained Chinese technocrats who assumed important positions in the party and government bureaucracies.

As a result of the first reform, KMT membership became over 70 percent Taiwanese, and the percentage of Taiwanese party and government officials grew to over 50 percent. The process of Taiwanization —which has yet to be fully implemented, especially in the military and security agencies—was highly important, because it helped to link the long-term interests of the Taiwanese and the KMT more closely. The

9

KMT is no longer a party dominated by Chinese from the mainland; its fate lies equally in the hands of Chinese from Taiwan.

The introduction of Western-trained technocrats into positions of power and responsibility in the government and party was also critical to the reform of Taiwan's political system. Many of these individuals used their positions to recommend and implement political reform. In addition, a significant number of overseas Chinese from the United States and other Western countries have returned to Taiwan to assume high-ranking posts. These individuals too have played an important liberalizing role in Taiwan's politics.

Elections. The practice of democracy on Taiwan has evolved upward from the grass-roots level. Local contested elections (township, city, and provincial) were first held in 1950–1951 and have been held regularly ever since. Voter turnout at local elections rarely falls below 70 percent of the registered voters, and Taiwanese win virtually every seat.[6] Candidates have included representatives from various factions within the KMT, independents, and other political parties (before 1986, the Young China party and the China Democratic Socialist party).

In elections for county magistrates and city mayors held in 1951, 1954, 1957, 1960, 1964, 1968, 1972, 1977, 1981, and 1985, the KMT won between 80 and 100 percent of the seats. The KMT also won between 70 and 85 percent of the seats in the Provincial Assembly elections of 1957, 1960, 1963, 1968, 1972, 1977, 1981, and 1985. In elections for the Taipei City Council in 1969, 1973, 1977, 1981, and 1985, the KMT won between 75 and 92 percent of the seats. And in the 1981 and 1985 Kaohsiung City Council elections, the KMT won 76 percent of the seats.[7]

Although local elections were instituted early on Taiwan, national elections have posed a major dilemma for the Republic of China. On the one hand, the KMT wants to democratize the political system as part of its program to make Taiwan a model province. On the other hand, the KMT has been reluctant to allow meaningful elections on Taiwan for the National Assembly, Legislative Yuan, and Control Yuan because these elected bodies are said to represent all of China, not just Taiwan.[8]

The dilemma was set aside temporarily by martial law provisions permitting those elected to national bodies on the mainland to continue to hold office without reelection on Taiwan. Over the years, this inevitably resulted in the ossification of the legislative bodies and their progressive irrelevance to central governmental politics. Under these circumstances, the executive branch of government assumed control of policy with few checks and balances from elected representatives.

To increase the vitality of the elected bodies and to reflect more accurately the importance of Taiwan to the ROC, a series of "supplementary" elections were held in 1969, 1972–1973, 1975, 1980, 1983, and 1986 to expand the size of Taiwan's representation in the Legislative Yuan, Control Yuan, and National Assembly. About 80 percent of the newly elected representatives to the Legislative Yuan, the most important of the elected bodies, were Taiwanese.

In the 1969 supplementary elections for fifteen National Assembly seats and eleven Legislative Yuan seats, the KMT won all assembly seats and eight (72 percent) of the legislative seats. During the 1972–1973 elections, the KMT won forty-three of the fifty-three contested National Assembly seats (81 percent) and forty-one of the fifty-one Legislative Yuan seats (80 percent) available for election. In the 1975 supplementary elections for fifty-two seats in the Legislative Yuan, the KMT won forty-two seats (81 percent). Most of the other seats were won by independent candidates. Very few seats were captured by the two officially sanctioned but largely ineffective parties competing with the KMT, the Young China party and the China Democratic Socialist party.

Under martial law, the formation of new political parties on Taiwan was not permitted. As a means of ensuring a united China under a strong KMT leadership, the KMT adopted the policy of "no party outside the party." This, of course, did not prevent the emergence of various factions within the KMT, many of which were based on local family alliances. These were especially strong in rural and southern Taiwan.

Beginning in 1977, however, a new factor was introduced into Taiwan's politics: more open competition between KMT and non-KMT candidates. Opposition to the KMT took the form of nonparty independents, or *tangwai* (literally, "outside the party"). Although the *tangwai* labored under martial law restrictions and were very disorganized and faction ridden, the *tangwai* nonetheless made an impressive showing.

In the 1977 elections, for instance, the *tangwai* captured 27 percent of the Provincial Assembly seats (up 12 percent for independents from the 1968 elections and 6 percent from the 1972 elections), 20 percent of the county magistrate and city mayoral seats (up 5 percent from 1968 and 100 percent from the 1972 elections), and 16 percent of the Taipei City Council seats (double the amount from previous elections in 1969 and 1973). The unexpected, strong showing of the *tangwai* caused a major reaction within the KMT, with some leading party reformers receiving blame.

Another step toward meaningful political competition in Taiwan's

11

politics occurred during the 1980 supplementary elections for seventy-six seats in the National Assembly and ninety-seven seats in the Legislative Yuan. The elections were held in the wake of the January 1, 1979, derecognition of the ROC by the United States and the Kaohsiung riot in December 1979. In that incident, a *tangwai* rally promoting human rights turned into a major riot (the responsibility for which is still in dispute) in the southern port city of Kaohsiung. Several policemen were seriously injured, and a number of major opposition leaders were arrested and sentenced to lengthy prison terms by military courts. This riot, plus an earlier one in Chungli, a small town in central Taiwan, became well-known incidents marking the confrontations of the *tangwai* with the KMT.[9]

In preparation for the 1980 elections, progressive KMT elements worked with various *tangwai* groups to evolve a set of ground rules to permit a more meaningful election process. The resulting Public Officials Election and Recall Law of May 1980 clearly favored the KMT, but it also provided for much greater freedom in campaigning for the opposition. Still banned by martial law from forming a political party, many of the opposition organized into a loose association with a common platform. Included in the platform were the following demands:

- More seats in the National Assembly, Legislative Yuan, and Control Yuan should be placed up for elections.
- Popular elections should be held for the governor of Taiwan Province and the mayors of Taipei and Kaoh-siung.
- More Taiwanese should be appointed to government positions.
- New political parties should be allowed to form.
- The scope of freedom of press, speech, and assembly should be broadened.
- Campaigning for elections should be less restricted.
- The Temporary Provisions should be abolished.
- Earlier political trials should be reviewed and most or all political prisoners released.
- The KMT should relinquish many of the powers and prerogatives that in other political systems belong to the government and not to a political party.

In spite of the restrictions placed on campaigning, the 1980 elections were hotly contested. Voter turnout was about 66 percent. The KMT backed forty-two candidates for the National Assembly and thirty-eight for the Legislative Yuan but won sixty-one seats in the National Assembly (80 percent of the contested seats) and seventy-nine seats in the Legislative Yuan (81 percent of the seats).[10]

As a group, the *tangwai* did not make a very good showing as a percentage of seats won (18 percent in the National Assembly and 16.5 percent in the Legislative Yuan); however, several individual *tangwai* received the highest number of votes of any of the candidates.

Competition between the KMT and the *tangwai* became even more open in the December 1983 supplementary elections for ninety-eight Legislative Yuan seats.[11] Voter participation was over 63 percent. The KMT captured eighty-three seats (85 percent), two went to the Young China party, one to the China Democratic Socialist party, and twelve (12 percent) went to others, including six to *tangwai* candidates. Although the KMT won 85 percent of the seats, it received only 73 percent of the total vote. The *tangwai* and other candidates won 27 percent of the vote but landed only 15 percent of the seats. The reason for this phenomenon was that the KMT was highly organized, while the independents were badly split between various factions. As in the 1980 elections, several *tangwai* candidates received the largest number of votes.

The next major supplementary election took place in December 1986.[12] In a significant step in the evolution of democracy on Taiwan, this election saw the emergence of a genuine (but as yet illegal) opposition party to the KMT: the Democratic Progressive party.

The election took place during a period of major political reform initiated by President Chiang Ching-kuo. At his urging, the KMT created a special task force in April 1986 to study the implementation of political reform in five key areas:

- lifting the emergency decree that activated martial law
- legalizing the formation of new political organizations
- strengthening the system of local self-government
- reinvigorating the Legislative Yuan
- internal reform of the KMT

Impatient with the progress of the task force, yet convinced that trends toward political liberalization were irreversible, the *tangwai* formally organized into the Democratic Progressive party in September 1986. Although this was technically an illegal act, the government decided not to intervene. The next month, President Chiang made the dramatic announcement to *Washington Post* chairman Katharine Graham that the ROC would soon lift martial law and allow new political parties to be formed.

In November 1986, the DPP adopted a platform that included the following major points:

- allow all residents of Taiwan to determine Taiwan's future; oppose any talks between the KMT and Communists on this issue as a violation of the principle of self-determination by the people of Taiwan
- cease confrontation between the two sides of the Taiwan Strait, which should compete with each other on an equal footing to preserve peace in the region
- adopt more flexible and active measures to rejoin the United Nations (The ROC lost its seat to the PRC as representative of China in 1971)
- cut the size of the nation's armed forces and shorten the length of compulsory military service
- close down all existing nuclear power plants within ten years and develop alternative sources of energy
- adopt a national health insurance program and an unemployment insurance program covering all citizens

The most controversial items of the DPP platform were calls for Taiwan's self-determination and equal footing between Taiwan and the mainland. To many people, these terms were code words for an independent Taiwan. This aspect of the DPP platform was troubling to many, because advocating independence for Taiwan was an illegal act under martial law. The 1947 ROC Constitution considers Taiwan a province of China, although, technically, Article 4 of the Constitution gives the National Assembly the authority by resolution to redefine the territory of the Republic of China.[13] Perhaps more important, the PRC had repeatedly threatened to preempt, by military force if necessary, any move toward Taiwan's independence. Regardless of its legal and security implications, the issue of self-determination played an uncertain role in the DPP's performance in the December 1986 elections.

After a hard-fought campaign, both the KMT and the DPP justifiably claimed victory in the elections. In the National Assembly, eleven of twenty-five DPP candidates were elected with 19 percent of the popular vote; 68 of 102 KMT candidates were elected with 68 percent of the vote. The remaining five assembly seats and 13 percent of the vote went to candidates from the China Democratic Socialist party (one seat) and independents (four seats). Thus, in the National Assembly, the KMT won 81 percent of the available seats, while the DPP won 13 percent, and others won 6 percent.

A total of a hundred seats were elected in the Legislative Yuan, of which the KMT won seventy-nine and the DPP won twelve. The KMT won 70 percent of the vote, and the DPP won 22 percent. The Young China party won two seats, the China Democratic Socialist party won one, and independents won six. The minor parties and independent candidates received 8 percent of the vote.

KMT candidates received a total of 69 percent of the 1986 vote and over 80 percent of the seats in the National Assembly and Legislative Yuan. DPP candidates received 21 percent of the vote and 15 percent of the seats in both bodies. The elections were the last national elections held before the December 1989 elections.

The Role of the Opposition

As revealed in interviews with KMT officials since 1986, some within the ruling party view the DPP and other oppositionists as distracting from Nationalist goals and even dangerous to ROC security. But, according to these sources, most KMT think opposition political parties play a useful role in providing needed checks and balances in the political system. Since the 1986 elections, however, the DPP has demonstrated both positive and negative influences on Taiwan's evolving democracy.

On the positive side, the DPP has become fairly effective as an opposition party in the Legislative Yuan and in presenting alternative proposals with popular appeal. It has been particularly successful in articulating consumer interests, environmental concerns, and the need for government accountability. Without question, the DPP has broken the "rubber-stamp" image the Legislative Yuan earned under KMT domination. Democracy on Taiwan has benefited thereby.

In contrast, many DPP legislators have been highly disruptive of parliamentary proceedings, using violence and parliamentary devices to freeze the legislative process for extended periods of time. DPP parliamentarians have also encouraged strikes and demonstrations. Many Chinese who value social harmony and government efficiency have been troubled by these developments.

Before the December 1989 elections, the DPP and other opposition candidates seemed capable of winning 20–25 percent of the total vote and 15–20 percent of available seats. But the DPP had serious internal weaknesses that limited its power and influence. One weakness was the DPP's small size. Membership rolls in late 1989 were said to contain only about 20,000 names. Other weaknesses included lack of coordination between leaders and their supporters, inexperience in politics, weak organization, too narrow a basis for appeal among the population, and ineffective central leadership.

The most damaging of these weaknesses was a badly split membership between those who wanted to work within the existing system to bring about gradual reform (the so-called "moderates," represented by Party Chairman Huang Hsin-chieh) and those who wanted to apply heavy pressure on the system to effect quick change (the "radicals," represented by National Assemblyman Hung Chi-chang). The issue of Taiwan's future deeply divided these two groups. Moderates wished to play down this issue to coordinate reforms with the KMT; many radicals demanded immediate moves toward Taiwan's independence.

The moderate faction, while a majority of the DPP, nonetheless was unable to gain control of the party, since moderate leaders were not unanimously accepted by the DPP membership and because the radicals controlled a highly active network of political journals. The radicals were also better able to mobilize members to participate in street demonstrations in support of DPP programs. This gained attention in the electronic media, otherwise inaccessible to the DPP because of KMT control of these channels of communication. Although a minority, radical DPP elements forced moderate opposition leaders to adopt confrontational tactics at times to ensure their political survival.

Not surprisingly, the actions of the DPP caused intense debates within the KMT over how best to handle the opposition. As disclosed in interviews since 1986, some KMT members felt that the DPP were little more than common criminals and that they posed a greater threat to Taiwan's security than the PRC. Some even perceived the DPP as a tool used by Beijing to destabilize the ROC's political system. Most KMT members, however, seemed to view the DPP as necessary for Taiwan's political evolution and believed that more reasonable opposition leaders would eventually emerge.

KMT policies toward the DPP reflected both cooperation and competition. On the one hand, in interviews with the author KMT leaders claimed that the party did not field candidates in certain districts for the 1986 elections to give the opposition greater opportunity to be elected. The KMT also worked hard to isolate radical members of the DPP by attempting to cooperate with more moderate DPP leaders. On the other hand, the KMT used its tremendous organizational strength and large pool of talented members to its advantage. One highly successful KMT tactic has been to adopt opposition proposals, such as environmental issues, when these appear to be popular with the public. Not surprisingly, the KMT has shown no indication that it wants to share significant power with any opposition party. Indeed, most KMT strategists believe the party will continue to dominate the government for the next twenty to thirty years.

Later Political Developments

On January 13, 1988, President Chiang Ching-kuo died, ushering in a new era of politics on Taiwan. Vice-President Lee Teng-hui, a native Taiwanese with a Ph.D. in agricultural economics from Cornell University, assumed the presidency according to the Constitution. Lee assured his countrymen that he would continue the democratization process begun by President Chiang.

Moving quickly in early February to fulfill his promise, Lee urged elderly legislative members to resign if they were unable to perform their duties. According to one calculation, this would have had the effect of retiring nearly two-thirds of Taiwan's 1,300 legislative members elected in 1947. In the same month Lee urged the KMT and the DPP to iron out their major differences. The new ROC president was clearly attempting to build a consensus between the KMT and the DPP over the future direction of democracy on Taiwan.

Whatever Lee's intentions, there were questions about whether he had the political power to implement democratic reform. Powerful conservative forces within the KMT believed the reforms were proceeding too fast and that Taiwan's stability was threatened. Moderates within the party backed Lee, however, and urged him to expand the reforms still further. They argued that reform was the only way to ensure the KMT's continued viability in the future.

The issues came to a head during the Thirteenth Party Congress in July 1988. After heated debate and much maneuvering behind the scenes, Lee and the moderates emerged victorious. The congress elected Lee chairman of the KMT, the first Taiwanese to hold that position. A new Central Standing Committee was also elected, of which sixteen were Taiwanese and fifteen were mainlanders, the first time Taiwanese had held a majority in that decision-making body. Like Lee, almost half the members had received advanced degrees in the United States. When Lee formed a new cabinet the following week, Taiwanese constituted eight of the thirteen newly appointed members.

In late 1988, the Legislative Yuan became the center of political attention as KMT and DPP members fought over numerous bills designed to reform Taiwan's political system. These bills included a proposal for the voluntary retirement of senior parliamentarians holding office since 1947 and a proposal to legalize the formation of new political parties on Taiwan.

The most serious confrontations between KMT and DPP legislators occurred over the Voluntary Retirement of Senior Parliamentarians Bill,

17

which called for the retirement of older officials, most of whom were elected on the mainland in 1947. The bill proposed paying each retiring official a pension of NT$3.74 million ($138,000).[14] DPP members strongly opposed the plan, demanding instead that a general election be held to force the lawmakers out of office without pension. Using parliamentary procedures and disruptive tactics, the DPP stopped all action in the Legislative Yuan as a way of forcing the KMT to drop the bill.

In December 1988, after several weeks of KMT efforts to convince the DPP to allow the bill to be considered, KMT legislators sent the bill into committee for discussion over heated DPP protests. The action sparked several melees in the Legislative Yuan. At various times DPP members stormed the speaker's podium, ripped out microphones, hurled chairs, and scuffled in the aisles with KMT legislators. Despite DPP protests, the voluntary retirement bill passed the Legislative Yuan and was signed by President Lee to become law on February 3, 1989.

In fact, the law signaled an important step toward democracy on Taiwan. As of early 1989, about 900 of the 1,000 members of the National Assembly (responsible for electing the president) and about 200 of the 300 members of the Legislative Yuan (responsible for passing legislation) were senior representatives frozen in office since 1947. Once these officials have retired, the legislative bodies will be composed mostly of representatives elected on Taiwan (see table 2–1).

At about the same time that the voluntary retirement bill was enacted, the KMT Central Standing Committee approved a plan to reduce the total members of the three legislative bodies to 579, less than half the current number. Under the plan, the National Assembly would have 375 deputies, the Legislative Yuan would have 150, and the Control Yuan would have 54 members.

There were several aspects of this plan. First, senior parliamentarians elected on the mainland in 1947 would be phased out through voluntary retirement. Those unable to exercise their responsibilities would be considered retired. Second, the number of parliamentarians representing ROC-controlled areas (Taiwan, Penghu, Kinmen, and Matsu) would increase in stages.[15] The number of Legislative Yuan seats open to election would increase from 100 in 1986 to 130 in 1989 and to 150 in 1992. The number of members of the National Assembly elected locally would increase from 84 in 1986 to 230 in 1992 and 375 in 1998. The number of locally elected members of the Control Yuan would increase from 32 to 54 in 1992. Third, the practice of allowing alternate deputies to fill National Assembly vacancies would be discontinued. And fourth, no seats would be reserved for mainland representatives in new elections.

18

TABLE 2–1
TYPES OF REPRESENTATION IN THE LEGISLATIVE BODIES IN THE REPUBLIC OF CHINA, 1989–1990

	Legislative Yuan, 1989	National Assembly, 1989	Control Yuan, 1989	Legislative Yuan, 1990
Directly elected by Taiwan people	54	57	0	78
Elected from groups				
Occupations	16	16	0	18
Women's groups	0	7	0	0
Aborigines	2	2	0	4
Fujien Province	1	2	0	1
Indirectly elected by Provincial Assembly and city councils	0	0	22	0
Total seats from Taiwan	73	84	22	101
Appointed from overseas Chinese	27	0	10	29
Elected in China in 1947	166	435	21	166
Alternate delegates appointed since 1947	0	277	0	0
Total seats from mainland	166	712	21	166
Total present membership	266	796	53	296
Percentage elected directly by Taiwan people	20.3	7.2	0.0	26.4
Percentage representing Taiwan (including indirect)	27.4	10.6	41.5	34.1

SOURCE: David Tsai, Testimony before the Subcommittee on Asian and Pacific Affairs, Committee on Foreign Affairs, U.S. House of Representatives, November 15, 1989.

19

If the plan goes forward, the character of Taiwan's legislative bodies will completely change over the next decade from representing primarily mainland China to representing primarily Taiwan.

Another important bill passed by the Legislative Yuan in early 1989 was the new Civic Organizations Law, legalizing new political parties on Taiwan for the first time. The law contained several major provisions insisted upon by the DPP, including: (1) the committee in charge of screening new parties should be directly under the Executive Yuan, not the Ministry of Interior; (2) no political party can appoint more than half the committee members; (3) to become legal, a new party has only to register, not seek prior approval; and (4) all political parties have equal access to the public mass media. The last provision was especially important to the DPP, because the KMT owns or controls most of Taiwan's electronic media.[16] The DPP, however, is well represented in the print media.

The Civic Organizations Law prohibited political parties from violating the Constitution, advocating communism, or supporting Taiwan's independence. The law stipulated that political groups must be organized and function in accordance with democratic principles. Two or more civic groups of the same nature can also be formed in the same geographical area and at the same administrative level. The law's provisions applied not only to political parties and organizations but also to professional and social organizations.

Since the passage of the law, more than forty political parties have been registered on Taiwan. With the exception of the KMT, the DPP, the China Democratic Socialist party, and the Young China party, political parties on Taiwan tend to reflect the interests of specialized groups such as labor, business, environmentalists, and Chinese nationalists. Some of the new parties include the Labor party, Worker's party, China Tatung Democratic party, China Hung Ying Patriotic party, China Democratic party, China Democratic Justice party, China Republican party, China United party, China New Socialist party, China Popular party, China Chungho party, China Unification party, Unification Democratic party, and China Loyal Virtue party.

On June 1, 1989, Premier Yu Kuo-hwa retired and was replaced by Lee Huan, considered a political reformer. At the same time, another important reform leader within the KMT, James Soong, was named secretary-general of the Kuomintang. Soong, who has a Ph.D. from Georgetown University, said at the time of his appointment that the most urgent task facing the KMT was to adjust the party's structure and to rejuvenate its spirit to make it more responsible and efficient. He said that, under his direction, the two major goals of the party would be to better reflect public opinion in government policies and to strengthen the party's organizational and mobilizing capabilities. Soong planned to hold regular meetings with government officials to ensure closer party-government coordination.[17]

A further indication of ROC and KMT policy direction came from President Lee Teng-hui in his address to the Second Plenum of the Thirteenth KMT Party Congress in June 1989. President Lee pointed out that the newly passed Civic Organizations Law legalized a competitive, multiparty system in the ROC. This would force the KMT to compete with new ideas and an efficient work attitude. As an urgent task, Lee called for the review and revision of the "Temporary Provisions" under which martial law was declared and which continued to give extraordinary powers to the ROC president. Many believed the continued existence of the Temporary Provisions constituted an obstacle to democracy. During his term in office, Lee has shifted ROC policy priorities from economic growth to social stability and a more equitable distribution of wealth.[18]

The leadership team of President Lee Teng-hui, Premier Lee Huan, and Secretary-General James Soong promised to usher in an even more liberal era on Taiwan.[19] But the immediate challenge for the new KMT leaders was the December 1989 elections.

21

3

The Elections

The December 2, 1989, elections were the first to be held since the lifting of martial law, and they were the first since the legalization of additional opposition parties to the KMT. Moreover, an exceptionally large number of seats were open for competition, along with a large number of candidates seeking them. It was also the first time that most of the candidates were selected through primaries.

But there were more fundamental issues involved. Over the past decade, Taiwan's political environment has changed dramatically. One systemic change has been the gradual withdrawal of the KMT as the coordinating link overseeing the island's political, economic, and social institutions. From 1949 until the late 1980s, the KMT provided the sole network of power that energized and directed Taiwan's entire body politic.

With the lifting of martial law and the greater separation of party and government, the unifying role played by the KMT has rapidly diminished. As a result, people on Taiwan are becoming increasingly self-reliant and independent. Special interest groups—labor, students, farmers, business, even the homeless—are organizing themselves to demand their rights. These groups have tried various tactics to articulate their views and win services, including a limited use of violence. To some extent the DPP has worked against this process of political maturation through its highly visible confrontations with the KMT.

Some on Taiwan view the spectacle of the scores of major protests and demonstrations since 1987 as a flowering of democracy and freedom. Often, these individuals criticize the government for not liberalizing fast enough. Others, more accustomed to stability on Taiwan, believe that society is on the verge of getting out of control. They often blame the KMT for failing to maintain social order.

There was widespread hope on Taiwan that the December 1989

elections would provide a clear judgment about who had been right and who had been wrong in the heated policy debates over the past three years. Many hoped that the test of popular will would determine how Taiwan was to be governed over the next decade and what direction Taiwan should take in its future development.

The elections were also seen as an opportunity to judge what to preserve and what to discard from the old system. Despite fundamental changes in Taiwan's political environment, the political structure of the island had remained largely in place, along with many government bureaucrats. The old structure and bureaucracy had many strengths, but many policy areas were also outdated and badly in need of change.

The elections were perceived as an opportunity to introduce new blood into the political system to counter conservative forces still in the government. Many hoped the Legislative Yuan would become a source of innovative ideas and a force for continued change. After the elections, the Legislative Yuan would have a total of 296 members. Of these, 166 or 56 percent would be senior legislators, most of whom were elected on the mainland in 1947. Of the remainder, 78 members or 26 percent of the Legislative Yuan would be representatives elected on Taiwan. The number of overseas Chinese legislators would be 29, or 10 percent; and representatives of professional and other groups would total 23, or 8 percent.

Since many senior parliamentarians were expected to retire within a few months after the elections, the percentages of various types of delegates in the Legislative Yuan would soon change dramatically in favor of those elected on Taiwan. For this reason, many voters felt that legislators elected in the 1989 contest would possess exceptional power to change the character of the Legislative Yuan and to make a significant impact on Taiwan's political future.

All in all, the December 1989 elections were viewed as a major test for democracy on Taiwan. Observers believed the elections would test the voters, the country's policies and politicians, government officials, and the existing political structure. Most of all, the elections would test society itself to see if democracy could really work on Taiwan.

The Electoral Process

As noted previously, 293 seats were open in the December 1989 elections, including 101 seats in the Legislative Yuan, 77 seats in the Taiwan Provincial Assembly, 51 seats in the Taipei City Council, 43 seats

23

in the Kaohsiung City Council, 16 county magistrate seats, and 5 mayoral seats.

In county magistrate and mayoral races on Taiwan, a single winner is chosen by a plurality of votes—an election process like that in the United States. Taiwan, however, has a single-vote, multimember electoral system for the Legislative Yuan, the Taiwan Provincial Assembly, and Taipei and Kaohsiung city councils. Under this system, each district has a certain number of seats (usually determined by population), which are won by candidates receiving the most votes.

For the Legislative Yuan, 302 candidates vied for 101 three-year seats in twenty-six geographic districts and a number of functional group constituencies. The geographic districts elected 79 members of the Legislative Yuan, whereas the functional groups elected 22 legislators. The geographic districts included the twenty-one counties and cities of Taiwan province,[20] one for the off-shore islands of Kinmen (Quemoy) and Matsu (considered part of Fujian Province), and two each for Taipei and Kaohsiung cities (considered administrative equivalents to a province).

The functional groups included farmers and laborers (both of which elected five representatives to the Legislative Yuan); industrial, commercial, education, and fishermen groups (all of which elected two representatives); and aborigine groups (two representatives each from mountain and nonmountain areas) (see table 3–1).

All seventy-seven seats in the Taiwan Provincial Assembly were up for election. Provincial assemblymen serve four-year terms. Competing for the seats were 157 candidates, seeking election in the twenty-one geographic districts of Taiwan Province (see table 3–2). As in the Legislative Yuan, candidates ran in single-vote, multimember district races.

Members of the Taipei City Council and the Kaohsiung City Council were also elected through single-vote, multimember elections. In the case of Taipei, a hundred candidates ran for all fifty-one seats in the council in citywide elections. In the Kaohsiung race, ninety-four candidates competed for all forty-three seats in citywide elections. Council members serve three-year terms.

To win in a single-vote, multimember district, a candidate must be among the top few contestants in number of votes received. The system spawns its own peculiar election strategies. To win the maximum number of seats in a given district, a party must estimate the number of votes it can expect, calculate the optimum number of candidates that can win with those votes, and then attempt to persuade prospective voters to

TABLE 3–1
REPRESENTATION BY GROUP IN THE LEGISLATIVE YUAN
FOR THE ELECTION OF DECEMBER 1989

Group	Seats	Candidates
Professional		
Commerce	2	11
Education	2	6
Farmers	5	12
Fishermen	2	4
Industrial	2	5
Laborers	5	27
Aborigines		
Nonmountain areas[a]	2	6
Mountain areas[b]	2	5
Overseas Chinese		
Asia		
Hong Kong, Macao	5	61
Northeast Asia	2	16
Other Asian regions	6[c]	43
Africa	1	11
Central and South America	1	18
Europe	2	28
North America	6[d]	124
Pacific	1	11
Global	5[e]	—

a. For the Provincial Assembly, two candidates from the north ran for one seat, and two candidates from the south ran for a seat.
b. For the Provincial Assembly, five candidates ran for two seats.
c. One of the global seats was reserved for an additional representative from other Asian regions, raising the total to seven seats.
d. One of the global seats was reserved for an additional representative from North America, raising the total to seven seats.
e. Global representatives were to be chosen from the above registered candidates; one of the five seats was reserved for North America; one of the five seats was reserved for other Asian regions.
SOURCE: Author.

TABLE 3–2
Competition for Contested Seats in the Taiwan Provincial Assembly, 1989

Geographic District	Number of Seats	Number of Candidates
Changhua County		
Magistrate	1	3
Legislature	4	13
Provincial Assembly	6	16
Chiayi County		
Magistrate	1	3
Legislature	2	6
Provincial Assembly	3	6
Hsinchu County		
Magistrate	1	2
Legislature	1	3
Provincial Assembly	2	5
Hualien County		
Magistrate	1	2
Legislature	1	4
Provincial Assembly	1	2
Ilan County		
Magistrate	1	3
Legislature	2	4
Provincial Assembly	2	6
Kaohsiung County		
Magistrate	1	3
Legislature	4	8
Provincial Assembly	5	7
Miaoli County		
Magistrate	1	3
Legislature	2	4
Provincial Assembly	3	5
Nantou County		
Magistrate	1	3
Legislature	2	7
Provincial Assembly	3	5

TABLE 3–2 (continued)

Geographic District	Number of Seats	Number of Candidates
Penghu County		
Magistrate	1	1
Legislature	1	2
Provincial Assembly	1	2
Pingtung County		
Magistrate	1	2
Legislature	3	6
Provincial Assembly	4	8
Taichung County		
Magistrate	1	2
Legislature	4	12
Provincial Assembly	6	13
Tainan County		
Magistrate	1	2
Legislature	4	10
Provincial Assembly	5	8
Taipei County		
Magistrate	1	6
Legislature	11	29
Provincial Assembly	10	19
Taitung County		
Magistrate	1	5
Legislature	1	6
Provincial Assembly	1	1
Taoyuan County		
Magistrate	1	4
Legislature	4	8
Provincial Assembly	6	11
Yunlin County		
Magistrate	1	4
Legislature	3	7
Provincial Assembly	4	7
Chiayi City		
Mayor	1	7
Legislature	1	3
Provincial Assembly	1	3

(Table continues)

TABLE 3–2 (continued)

Geographic District	Number of Seats	Number of Candidates
Hsinchu City		
Mayor	1	2
Legislature	1	6
Provincial Assembly	1	3
Keelung City		
Mayor	1	3
Legislature	1	2
Provincial Assembly	2	3
Taichung City		
Mayor	1	2
Legislature	3	12
Provincial Assembly	4	11
Tainan City		
Mayor	1	4
Legislature	2	9
Provincial Assembly	3	6

SOURCE: Author.

divide their votes evenly among these candidates.

With its long experience with the electoral system and its superior organization, training, recruitment, and financial resources, the KMT possesses a significant advantage over the DPP and other political parties in its ability to maximize the number of its winning candidates in each district. In contrast, the single-vote, multimember electoral system makes it fairly easy for an attractive candidate to win a seat. Independents, therefore, have long enjoyed a certain degree of success in Taiwan's elections. More recently, the *tangwai* and the DPP have proven capable of fielding an impressive array of colorful individual candidates who often win more votes than individual KMT candidates. The combination of the relative strengths of the KMT and the opposition has resulted in the phenomenon, noted earlier, that the KMT wins a larger percentage of seats than percentage of votes and that the DPP wins a larger percentage of votes than percentage of seats in single-vote, multimember races.

Election Regulations

The rules governing the December 1989 elections were contained in a revised Public Functionaries Election and Recall Bill passed by the Legislative Yuan on January 26, 1989, and signed into law by President Lee Teng-hui on February 3. This was the second revision of the original election law of 1980. The purpose of the 1989 revision was to bring the law into accord with the Civic Organizations Law permitting the formation of new political parties and to respond to public demands for greater participation in politics.

Under the new election law, the Central Election Commission was placed under the Executive Yuan and made the supreme decision-making body responsible for elections. Lower-level election commissions were also established. No more than 50 percent of the commission's members could belong to one party. The KMT, the Young China party, and the China Democratic Socialist party appointed representatives to the various election commissions. The DPP refused to do so on the grounds that it wanted more seats. The DPP demanded at least one-third of the fifteen to nineteen seats on the Central Election Commission, for example.

The election law stipulated that all ROC nationals who had attained the age of twenty years had the right to vote, except those declared incompetent or those whose civil rights had been revoked and not reinstated. Individuals could vote either in their domicile of origin or in the place where they resided for the past six months. If soldiers were able to get leave from their posts, they could vote as regular citizens at their place of birth or residence. There were no absentee ballots.

Although voters were encouraged to vote in their own district, they could vote elsewhere if they notified officials twenty-five days before the voting day. Members of occupational groups or women's groups were also expected to vote for representatives from these categories unless they notified authorities sixty days beforehand that they wished to vote for regional representatives. If an individual was a member of two groups, then he voted with the first group he joined unless he notified authorities beforehand. If he joined two groups at the same time, then he would vote for a regional representative.

Any elector who had attained the age of twenty-three could register for office (age thirty in the case of mayor), except those:

- who had committed treason or were convicted of sedition, graft, violence against other candidates, or bribery
- who were serving criminal sentences

- who were declared bankrupt and whose rights were not yet restored

In addition, military men and policemen on active duty, students, and persons handling election affairs could not be candidates. There were also educational requirements for candidates: a senior high school education for members of the Legislative Yuan, Provincial Assembly, and Taipei and Kaohsiung city councils and a junior college degree or a high school education with some professional experience for magistrate and mayoral candidates.

Other regulations specified the period during which candidates and parties were permitted to conduct campaign activities. As defined by the Central Election Commission, all candidates for election had to register between October 23 and October 30. Some 724 individuals registered; of these, 722 were judged qualified candidates by the commission.[21]

On November 16 those candidates deemed qualified to run for the Legislative Yuan were announced. They began their election activities on November 17 and continued through December 1. Campaigning was permitted between 7:00 A.M. and 10:00 P.M. Legislative Yuan candidates could hold privately sponsored political rallies from November 17 to November 23. From November 24 until December 1, only publicly sponsored rallies were allowed.

The list of qualified candidates for seats other than those for the Legislative Yuan were announced on November 21. These candidates could conduct election activities between November 22 and December 1, again between the hours of 7:00 A.M. and 10:00 P.M. Private rallies could be held between November 22 and November 26, while only public rallies could be held between November 27 and December 1.

The Election Commission determined the maximum amount of campaign expenditures for each office in each district based on a complex formula.[22] In Taipei County, for example, candidates for the Legislative Yuan could spend up to NT$7,192,000 ($266,370); candidates for the Provincial Assembly could spent up to NT$5,827,000 ($215,815); and candidates for the county magistrate position could spend up to NT$8,405,000 ($311,296).

Regulations also governed subsidies and political contributions. Candidates who received three-fourths of the minimum votes required to elect a public official in a certain electoral district were given NT$10 per vote as a subsidy from the election committee at the level at which they campaigned. Under the revised election law, no foreign contributions were permitted, but private contributions were allowed for the first time. An individual could contribute a maximum of NT$20,000 ($740) to a political candidate and NT$200,000 ($7,400) to a political party. Individual donations could not exceed 20 percent of the donor's yearly income before taxes. The maximum donation by businesses was NT$300,000 ($11,000) to candidates and NT$3 million ($110,000) to political parties. Donations could not exceed 10 percent of the business's annual income before taxes. All legal contributions were tax deductible.

Other regulations stipulated that each candidate could have only five sound trucks; their use had to be approved in advance. Campaign speeches could be given only during public and private campaign forums. No more than six candidate-sponsored meetings could be held during one day, and each meeting could last no more than two hours. In publicly sponsored rallies, each candidate could speak for only fifteen minutes. Demonstrations, signature drives, and firecrackers were not allowed. Campaign posters could be erected only within thirty meters of a campaign headquarters and could be put up only by the candidate or his staff. Using radio or television to broadcast campaign advertising was prohibited.

Candidates had to submit written platforms and newsletters to the Election Commission for approval. The platforms, as well as statements by the candidates and assistants, could not instigate persons to commit "offenses against the internal security or external security of the state," incite persons "to undermine social order with violence," or to commit other criminal offenses. As defined by the Central Election Commission, these prohibitions meant that platforms could not advocate Taiwan independence or the division of China and could not directly attack someone. The commission did authorize, however, a great deal of latitude in making policy recommendations regarding future relations between Taiwan and the mainland. Platforms could, for example, advocate improved relations across the Taiwan Strait or recommend that both sides join the United Nations, but platforms could not call for elections of a new parliament or the creation of a new constitution. If the platform was not approved, the candidate was asked to revise it. If the revision was still not acceptable, the Election Commission deleted the offending language from the platform.

Polling places were established in public buildings, schools, and other appropriate sites in the various districts. Upon completion of balloting, the poll site was turned into a ballot-opening station where ballots were counted aloud in the presence of the public and voting officials. Each candidate or political party was able to assign inspectors during the balloting and during the counting to ensure a fair and free election. The election of officials was conducted on the basis of universal suffrage, equality among citizens, and direct and secret ballots.

Punishments were specified for violations of the election and recall law. The law stipulated that candidates instigating persons to commit offense against the internal or the external security of the state would be punished by sentences of not less than seven years; inciting people to violence would be punishable by sentences of not less than five years; and committing other offenses would be punishable in accordance with relevant laws. Moreover, candidates or their assistants who violated the law during their campaign speeches would be dealt with according to the above rules. Stiff penalties were assigned to those who gave or accepted bribes or who interfered with the duties of election officials. Minor fines were assigned to such violations as placing posters in unauthorized locations.

Election Procedures

Elaborate safeguards ensured fair and free balloting. The ballots were printed under the supervision of inspection committees to see that the number printed corresponded to the number of constituents, with a specified number of extra copies in case ballots were damaged.

After printing, the ballots were sealed, transported to the designated polling places under guard, and turned over to the supervisor of the polling station. There, the ballots were recounted by election officials assigned to the voting place to guarantee the proper number. Afterward, the container was again sealed and watched until the morning of the elections.

An individual was permitted to vote when he presented his identification card, voter registration card, and personal "chop," or name seal. After his name was checked with a list of qualified registered voters in the district, his chop was then inscribed beside his name. The voter was given one or more ballots—one ballot for each office being filled in his district. He marked his ballots with a red seal in secret behind curtains and then dropped the ballot into an appropriately labeled opaque box. The entire process, except the actual voting behind a curtain, was open to scrutiny.

Polling stations were open from 8:00 A.M. until 5:00 P.M. (polls in Kinmen and Matsu opened at 7:30 A.M. and closed at 3:30 P.M.). At their close, the polls became vote-counting stations. Each ballot was held aloft for the public to see. Then the marked candidate's name was read aloud, and his vote was indicated on a large tally sheet taped to the wall. If the ballot was not marked correctly, it was declared void. If a member of the audience or one of the inspectors questioned a ballot, it was reexamined and a consensus reached among the examiners about whether it should be counted.

After all the votes at an individual polling station had been counted, three copies of the results were made—again before the public. One was posted outside the station, one copy and the ballots were kept locked in a safe, and one was sent under guard to the central vote-counting center for the office for which the election was held.

At the central vote-counting center, the results of the elections were put into a computer. The printout was checked against the original tally to ensure accuracy, and any corrections were put into the computer. The computer was connected to the Central Vote Counting Center in Taipei where the final tabulations were made. All these procedures were open to the public, and the results were televised from the Taipei vote-counting center. All candidates received the results from all the polling stations.

Primaries

Both the KMT and the DPP held primaries on July 23, 1989, to choose their respective candidates. This was the first time that primaries had been held on Taiwan. About 900,000 KMT members cast their ballots (46 percent of the total KMT membership of approximately 2.5 million),[23] while around 14,000 DPP members voted (70 percent of the total DPP membership of 20,000).

Kuomintang. The KMT primary was seen as a major step in the democratization of the ruling party. In the past, most KMT-sponsored candidates were chosen by the party leadership. During internal KMT discussions over whether to have primaries, a debate arose over the fundamental nature of the party. According to party officials interviewed, some KMT members argued that the party should retain a high degree of revolutionary spirit, because the mainland had not yet been recovered and Taiwan was not yet ready for complete democracy. Other members argued that the revolutionary phase of the party had passed and that now was the time to emphasize the democratic nature of the KMT.

The party leaders decided to proceed with the primaries because they wanted to involve all KMT members in the process of selecting party candidates. Their objective was to strengthen the representativeness and legitimacy of these candidates, thereby increasing their attractiveness to the general public at a time when open competition was becoming a major factor in winning elections. The primary, therefore, was intended to

33

help the KMT win more seats in the December elections.

A total of 670 KMT members ran in the primaries, competing for 222 party nominations in the December general elections. For the Legislative Yuan seats elected by the general public 164 KMT members competed, 90 for the Legislative Yuan seats elected by aborigine and professional groups, 153 for the Taiwan Provincial Assembly seats, 111 for the Taipei City Council seats, 71 for the Kaohsiung City Council seats, and 81 for the county magistrate and city mayoral seats.

To qualify to run in the primary, KMT members had to meet the legal requirements outlined in the revised election and recall law, plus have held nonpaid party posts and received endorsement from at least 0.5 percent of party members in county or city executive districts or 0.2 percent of party members in a legislative election district. Those running in the primary also signed a pledge to avoid bribery and violence and to refrain from making personal attacks during the December election campaign. Candidates solicited support during speeches at party-sponsored forums. Self-sponsored rallies were not permitted. Party officials were asked to remain aloof and not to favor one candidate over another.

On the whole, the KMT primaries were successful since 90 percent of the KMT-sponsored candidates in the general elections were selected in the primaries. The remainder of the candidates were chosen on the basis of the primaries and other considerations, such as the party leadership's assessment of their qualifications. Some selection was necessary because KMT rules specified that, to win, a candidate had to receive the most votes in elections in which voter turnout was at least 50 percent of eligible party voters. In several instances, voter turnout fell below 50 percent.

As a result of the primaries, the KMT sponsored 222 candidates in the December elections, including 71 candidates for the Legislative Yuan, 53 for the Taiwan Provincial Assembly, 44 for the Taipei City Council, 34 for the Kaohsiung City Council, and 20 for the mayoral and county magistrate slots.

According to data provided by the KMT, on average the candidates were middle-aged and highly educated. Eighteen had Ph.D. degrees, 41 had master's degrees, and 119 (54 percent) had graduated from college. Thirty-three (15 percent) candidates were women. About half the nominees were incumbents; 181 (82 percent) were Taiwanese, and 41 (18 percent) were first- or second-generation mainlanders.

In addition to these 222 KMT-sponsored candidates, another 124 KMT members registered as candidates on their own in the general elections. These individuals did not win in the primaries, nor did the KMT request that they run. In fact, 13 faced expulsion from the party because they ran against officially sanctioned candidates for mayors and county magistrates.

Several problems arose with the KMT primaries. First, although the primaries were intended to increase the number of KMT victories in the December general elections, this did not occur. Second, while KMT officials denied the existence of a preferred list of candidates backed by party leaders, a few incidents of party interference in the primary process were reported. Third, several incidents of vote buying were alleged in certain districts. And fourth, special interest groups apparently were able to mobilize their members to secure nominations for favored candidates, irrespective of the candidates' appeal to voters at large.

Democratic Progressive Party. The DPP also held primaries to select its candidates. Before the primary process began, however, DPP chairman Huang Hsin-chieh publicized his own list of preferred candidates for county magistrates and city mayors. Some DPP candidates were talked into dropping out of the primaries because they were not on the preferred list.

The existence of the list became even more controversial because of major differences between two DPP factions. The Formosan faction, led by party chairman Huang Hsin-chieh, advocated a gradual change in the nation's political system. It emphasized democracy first and Taiwan's independence second. The Formosan faction believed that the DPP's emphasis on self-determination would scare away too many middle-class voters.

The New Movement faction, led by former DPP chairman Yao Chia-wen, regarded Taiwan's independence as its most important policy objective and a key campaign issue. More radical in its orientation than the Formosan faction, New Movement leaders believed in strong party discipline. Many wanted to purify the DPP of all not accepting its ideology. Most of the DPP incumbents belonged to the Formosan faction, whereas the New Movement was composed largely of political activists. For a time, the New Movement faction threatened to break away from the DPP, but this did not occur.

Despite these internal difficulties, the DPP primaries were generally successful in their purpose. The primaries resulted in the DPP nomination of 145 candidates, while 18 DPP members ran in the December elections on their own. The Formosan faction gained the largest number of positions for its candidates.

But the DPP primaries suffered criticisms as well. First, some questioned whether primaries were the best way to select DPP nominees, since DPP membership is extremely small in certain areas (some won primaries in which fewer than a hundred DPP voters participated). Second, some believed that factional politics within the DPP and alleged incidents of vote buying marred the opposition primary even more than that of the KMT. And third, since only the most active members of the DPP voted in the primaries, the New Movement faction might have won a disproportionately large number of party nominations.

The KMT Platform and Election Strategy

The KMT began preparations for the December 1989 elections two years earlier. As the election neared, many party officials could see that the elections would redefine the KMT's role in society, determine its relations with other political parties, judge the wisdom of its reforms, and greatly influence the future of the ROC.

To the KMT, the elections represented a new allocation of power and resources. If the party won a sufficiently large number of votes and seats, then the reforms instituted since 1986 would be vindicated. If the KMT did poorly in the elections, then blame would be laid either on remaining hard-liners within the party and government or on the reformers. If the hard-liners were blamed for the loss, then they would be forced to retire early. If the reformers were discredited, then they would lose power, creating an opportunity for conservatives to make a political comeback.

Most KMT analysts expected the results of the 1989 elections to be similar to those of the 1986 elections. Analysts believed that the Nationalists would win 70–80 percent of the vote, while the DPP and other parties would win 20–30 percent. But this degree of success could not be taken for granted. Despite the superior organization and overwhelming size advantages enjoyed by the KMT over other political parties, more than 75 percent of Taiwan's voters are not KMT members.

To win 70 percent of the vote, the KMT pursued a straightforward strategy of appealing to voters on the basis of its past accomplishments, particularly since 1986 when President Chiang Ching-kuo initiated major reforms, and promises to achieve even more success in the future.

The KMT prepared an extensive platform for the 1989 elections.[24] Promising to carry out further political reform and to achieve constitutional democracy, the ruling party said it would:

- strengthen the ROC parliament to make it fully representative, more capable, and vigorous

36

- bolster the system of local government
- revise the Temporary Provisions
- promote the rule of law and safeguard human rights
- improve law and order and reduce crime
- raise the quality of government and root out corruption

The KMT promised to expand the ROC's diplomatic horizons by:

- conducting foreign relations on the basis of practicality, flexibility, and forward-looking actions
- widening ROC participation in international organizations
- promoting international cooperation and exchange, including additional assistance to developing countries
- assisting overseas Chinese in their cultural and economic development, as well as their anti-Communist movements

The KMT platform pledged to strengthen the nation's defense and to ensure national security. Specifically, the KMT said it would:

- achieve a national consensus on the level and type of defense needed for Taiwan
- modernize the armed forces around the concept of an elite force
- increase defense preparedness of Kinmen, Matsu, Taiwan, and Penghu
- create opportunities to recover the mainland and develop anti-Communist forces there
- further develop defense technology and establish an independent defense system

The KMT called for the creation of a new economic environment, including a more equitable distribution of wealth. Toward this end, the KMT promised to:

- expand public investment
- establish a fair and reasonable taxation system
- improve the nation's financial management system
- privatize more public enterprises
- upgrade industry, while assisting small and medium-sized businesses
- ensure fair trade and competition
- improve the nation's transportation and other infrastructure
- liberalize trade by expanding imports and diversifying export markets
- guarantee a stable energy supply

37

The KMT platform promised to improve the quality of public education and to emphasize moral education. In addition to increased funds for scientific and technological development, the KMT also promised to promote Chinese culture and modern ethics. The platform included proposals to establish a ministry of cultural affairs, to revive traditional Chinese culture and values, to implement a set of norms of social behavior for a modern society, to foster local culture, to help writers and artists, to improve the quality of mass communications, and to safeguard freedom of the press.

To promote social welfare, the KMT promised to:

- establish a health and welfare department, raise expenditures for health and welfare, and improve social services
- increase assistance to retired servicemen and the aborigines
- adopt more reasonable population growth and distribution policies
- complete a nationwide medicare system and promote a universal health insurance program
- enact a consumer protection law
- construct additional recreational facilities and improve national scenic spots

Regarding pollution and the nation's ecology, the KMT said it would better the quality of the environment, protect natural resources, improve the nation's environmental protection system, and strengthen the prevention and control of pollution.

To safeguard workers' rights and to promote harmony between labor and management, the KMT platform promised to establish a labor ministry, revise the Minimum Wage Law and the Labor Union Law, reduce occupational hazards, implement regulations to facilitate labor and management coordination, and improve labor welfare.

The KMT said it would increase farmers' income and improve their welfare by establishing a ministry of agriculture, increasing investment in agriculture, stabilizing prices and making the marketing of farm products more efficient, limiting the import of foreign agricultural products when these hurt the interests of Taiwanese farmers, accelerating the development of the fishing industry, protecting forest resources, and supporting farmers' and fishermen's organizations.

Similar promises were made to protect women's rights. The KMT platform promised to uphold the equality of the sexes, expand opportunities for women, strengthen social welfare service for women, protect abused women, and encourage women to play a more active role in social service.

The KMT platform promised to promote the "Taiwan Experience" and to continue to work toward the reunification of China. The KMT said it would:

- support political democratization on mainland China to oppose the Communist dictatorship
- promote economic liberalization on the mainland, including the private ownership of property, the free enterprise system, and a market-oriented economic system
- promote social pluralization on the mainland, including respect for basic human rights and equal educational opportunity
- promote traditional Chinese values on the mainland and support opposition to Marxism-Leninism
- encourage more grass-roots exchanges across the Taiwan Strait and the creation of anti-Communist united fronts at home and abroad
- amend mainland trade policy to place equal emphasis on national security and economic benefits
- support racial minority groups in border areas fighting against the Communists
- publicize the Taiwan Experience as a means of achieving a "reunified, democratic, and prosperous new China"

The KMT platform was a remarkable document in that it committed the ruling party to a vast range of progressive policies. Essentially, the KMT was asking voters to continue to support the party because of its past success in modernizing Taiwan, the broad reforms it had introduced since 1986, and assurances that if it remained in power, the KMT would implement even more rapid reform in the future.

Despite the great advantages enjoyed by the KMT, the party was often clearly on the defensive in the elections. It was plagued by negative images caused in large part by four factors. First, the KMT suffered from the continued presence of superannuated statesmen in the National Assembly and Legislative Yuan. Second, the KMT was criticized for the lack of separation between the party, the government, and the military. Third, the KMT's image was damaged by its inability to solve the most visible, pressing problems facing Taiwan in 1989: growing pollution, grid-locked traffic, and a sharp rise in crime. And fourth, many KMT candidates were tarnished by frequent allegations of bribery and vote buying.

DPP Platform and Strategy

While the KMT was on the defensive in the elections to preserve its existing base of voter support and seats, the DPP was on the offensive to win a larger role in Taiwan's politics. As in the case of the KMT, the elections were deemed vital to the future of the DPP and a major determinant of DPP policies. The elections, it was thought, would test the public's approval of the DPP's performance. Specifically, the elections would signal whether the people of Taiwan wanted the DPP to continue its confrontational tactics or whether the public wanted the DPP to play a more cooperative role as "loyal opposition" to the KMT.

Because of internal disagreement over policy, the DPP did not publish a specific platform for the December elections. Nonetheless, the DPP's policy suggestions, first published in November 1986 and modified in April 1988, contained principles and proposals covering most areas of public policy.[25]

The DPP advocated a political order based on democracy and freedom. It held that the nation should rest on the free will of the majority of the people and should respect the principle of self-determination. It stated that the government should protect basic human rights, popular sovereignty, division of power, rule of law, judiciary independence, and equal status for all political parties. The DPP claimed that these principles had been seriously distorted by the Temporary Provisions, but while the provisions were in effect, the government should:

- maintain human dignity and basic human rights
- ensure that laws comply with the people's wishes
- set up a sound system for division of power and checks and balances at all levels of government and between the central and the local governments
- ensure freedom, equality, and democracy for all political parties
- protect freedom of assembly and association
- protect freedom of the press, including independence of newspapers, broadcasting stations, and television from the government
- ensure rule of law and independence of the judiciary
- establish a neutral administrative system, independent of control by any political party
- enable the Legislative Yuan to supervise the government's emergency decrees and recognize the right of the people to resist emergency decrees

The DPP supported a balanced economic and financial administration in which Taiwan would play a role as a viable member of the international economic community but would pursue independent national policies enabling the people to share the fruits of the nation's economic growth. To accomplish this, the DPP suggested that the government:

- respect private property and create a better investment environment
- encourage stable economic growth by protecting Taiwan's businessmen from fluctuations in overseas markets
- ensure full employment
- assist small and medium-sized enterprises
- promote balanced development of every sector of the economy
- allow private investment in state-owned enterprises and place the enterprises under the supervision of central and local councils
- develop agricultural and fishery resources
- improve the financial, taxation, and monetary systems

The DPP also called for a fair and open social welfare system. This meant the establishment of a harmonious and stable social system, the pursuit of a welfare state, the institution of a social security system, the improvement of working conditions, the establishment of democratic controls over state-owned enterprises, and the implementation of a more effective population control policy.

For educational reform, the DPP proposed the removal of political intervention in the school system, the allocation of more money for education, the creation of additional vocational education schools, and political neutrality and academic freedom for students and faculty. The DPP also advocated equal development of grass-roots and modern culture, the maintenance of cultural diversity, and efforts to reduce consumer-oriented and entertainment-oriented cultural styles.

The DPP called for peaceful and independent defense and foreign policies. The DPP suggested that the government:

- develop its relations with other countries based on the principles of equality, reciprocity, independence, and self-determination
- assume more flexible and active measures to handle problems related to Taiwan's status in the international community
- seek to resolve international disputes by peaceful means, including support for worldwide disarmament talks, control of military equipment, and destruction of nuclear and chemical weapons
- cut the size of the military and upgrade its quality through more purchases of air and naval weapons systems; diversify the sources of military procurement; and strengthen domestic production of weapons
- place the armed forces, which should be politically neutral, under the jurisdiction of civilian government authorities, including the Legislative Yuan

41

Regarding the issue of Taiwan's future, the DPP said that the government should allow all residents of Taiwan an equal opportunity to determine the future of Taiwan and its political affiliation. The governments on the two sides of the Taiwan Strait should cease confrontations, moving toward a satisfactory solution to the problem based on the principles of humanity, equality, peace, and the interests of the people of Taiwan. The DPP opposed any talks on this issue that contradicted the principle of self-determination. The DPP argued that as long as the living standards and social systems of the two sides of the Taiwan Strait are in sharp contrast, the authorities on both sides should give priority to improving the living standards of their people and should not create tensions.

According to DPP campaign officials in their briefings to delegations of foreign observers, four critical issues dominated the 1989 elections. First was the question of whether Taiwan was to be democratic. If so, the officials argued, then a general election should determine all legislative seats and the president as well. Moreover, the military, the security forces, and the civil service should pledge loyalty to the country, not to the KMT, and the judiciary should not be under the control of the KMT.

Second was the issue of corruption in the government and the KMT. According to the DPP, corruption had worsened over the past three years because of a thirst for money in society, reflected in increased bribery, officials' playing the lottery, and various money-making schemes leading to trouble for several KMT and government officials.

Third was the issue of government inefficiency. According to the DPP, this inefficiency was evidenced in major unresolved problems such as traffic, pollution, and crime; inflation and taxation; health insurance; and privatization of government-owned businesses.

Last was the issue of whether a new constitution should replace the Constitution of 1947 enacted on the mainland. The DPP argued that the 1947 Constitution is unrealistic, because it seeks to represent all China, not the territory actually under the control of the ROC.

On the sensitive issue of Taiwan's independence, DPP officials emphasized four points. First, people living on Taiwan have the exclusive right to determine their future relationship with China. Second, although the DPP advocates self-determination, it does not specifically suggest what that decision should be. Third, the people of Taiwan should be allowed to discuss their future, whether it be independence, unification, or some other arrangement between Taiwan and China. And fourth, DPP officials stressed that there was no urgency to make a decision on the self-determination issue.

As already indicated, significant differences of opinion existed among DPP candidates over the issue of Taiwan's independence. A few weeks before the elections, thirty-two DPP candidates from the New Movement faction formed the New Nation Alliance, which openly advocated a "new nation, a new parliament, and a new constitution." The alliance platform was deemed illegal by the Central Election Commission, but members publicly campaigned for a new nation anyway.

Other DPP members criticized the alliance's call for an independent Taiwan on the grounds that advocating independence was impractical and dangerous for both the DPP and Taiwan. Perhaps in response to this sentiment, many New Movement candidates toned down their advocacy of Taiwan's independence to attract a broader range of voter support for the party and for themselves.

The DPP insisted that the current election system was fundamentally unfair, because even if opposition candidates won 100 percent of the popular vote, they would win only about one-third of the seats in the Legislative Yuan. Having no hope of winning a majority there, DPP strategy focused on winning county magistrate and city mayoral posts. This important strategic decision has potentially major consequences for Taiwan.

Local executives on Taiwan maintain a large discretionary power over budgets and implementation of national policies. County magistrates have the authority to raise money through bonds or lotteries, and they control zoning. The officials can decide whether a nuclear power plant should be built in the county. DPP strategists believed these areas of local control could be used to bargain with the KMT on national policy. They believed that if the DPP could win a large number of local seats, then it could exert a major national influence by creating fear in the KMT of a split between local and central governments.

The DPP also hoped that by winning local offices, its candidates could demonstrate their competence to voters. Such a demonstration could take place only where officials exercised real power over budget and planning. This was not the case in the Legislative Yuan. Winning local elections in 1989, therefore, would enable future DPP candidates to take more seats in subsequent contests. Believing that the Taiwanese people wanted a change from the KMT, the DPP expected that its local strategy could result in a major change in power in seven to twelve years. As more offices were occupied by DPP members, the KMT would splinter, and various factions would work with the DPP on specific issues.

Most DPP strategists did not think the KMT would willingly surrender power to the opposition. They expected the ruling party to stretch out political liberalization as far into the future as possible. Most DPP supporters believed the KMT must be forced to change.

To implement its local strategy, the DPP persuaded many of its best-known members, including incumbents in the Legislative Yuan, to run for local offices. Younger, less-experienced members were asked to run for the Legislative Yuan. The DPP assumed that the electorate would give the opposition party its "rightful" share of seats in the legislature, while voters would also elect a number of outstanding DPP candidates as magistrates or mayors. One DPP official estimated that the party could win ten of the twenty-one local executive positions through this strategy.

On a tactical level, individual DPP candidates—like most of their KMT rivals—emphasized local issues in their races. Local DPP candidates interviewed by the author said the keys to election were issues of immediate public concern such as traffic, the environment, education, housing, and unemployment. At the same time, however, these DPP candidates freely admitted their support for the independence of Taiwan. But few local candidates made independence a campaign issue.

According to DPP data, which differed somewhat from government counts, the DPP had a total of 148 candidates, including 51 candidates for the Legislative Yuan, 38 for the Provincial Assembly, 21 for the Taipei City Council, 21 for the Kaohsiung City Council, and 17 for county magistrates and mayors.

Information provided by the ROC Government Information Office said the DPP fielded a total of 163 candidates, including 57 for the Legislative Yuan, 43 for the Taiwan Provincial Assembly, 21 for the Taipei City Council, 24 for the Kaohsiung City Council, and 18 for county magistrates and city mayors. According to the government count, the DPP nominated 145 candidates, while 18 other DPP members ran on their own without party backing. In some cases, maverick DPP members faced expulsion from the party.[26]

Human Rights and Election Irregularities

Although without question Taiwan's human rights situation has vastly improved over that existing under martial law, several human rights problems worked to limit the prospects of a fair and free election.

Most of these were documented by the Clean Election Coalition (CEC), a newly formed volunteer organization modeled after the National Movement for Free Elections in the Philippines. Designed to focus attention on election abuses, the coalition was headed by a leading Taiwanese opposition figure, and its reports tended to be more critical of the KMT than of the DPP.

As for freedom of expression, the CEC noted that several magazines were suspended before the elections (such as the *New Movement* for advocating Taiwan's independence). Moreover, during the previous year several writers and publishers were accused of sedition for advocating Taiwan's independence (as in the case of Cheng Nan-jung, who committed suicide in protest) or for spreading rumors of a pending *coup d'état* by the military (as in the case of Chen Wei-tu, editor of *Democratic Progressive Weekly*). The Clean Election Coalition was especially critical of Taiwan's television news media, which were supposed to be neutral in the elections. The CEC claimed that television stations reported more favorably on certain KMT candidates than on others.

As for freedom of assembly, the CEC reported that some organizers of rallies that had turned violent were being held criminally liable, even though the organizers had neither advocated nor participated in the violence. Freedom of association may also have been abridged, when about a hundred organizations using "Taiwan" in their names had to add "Republic of China" or face disbandment and the possible imprisonment of their leaders. Members of the New Nation Alliance, which openly advocated independence for Taiwan, were subject to investigation for sedition.

A related concern was the restriction placed on the rights of former political prisoners. Many thousands had been arrested under martial law for activities now considered legal; yet the civil rights of many of these individuals had not been restored.

All these cases were relevant to the December elections, because those found guilty of serious crimes, especially sedition, could neither participate in the elections nor hold office if elected. Several DPP leaders were thus barred, including the current chairman, the general secretary of the party, and the previous chairman. DPP spokesmen pointed to this fact as evidence that the justice system was being used to punish the opposition or to limit its effectiveness.

In the weeks before the elections, the CEC reported several cases of violence that might have been politically motivated. These included the shooting death of an opposition leader in Kaohsiung, the burning of the Taichung headquarters of a DPP candidate for mayor, threats received by several KMT candidates, the serious gunshot injury of an independent candidate for the Legislative Yuan from Changhua County, the assault on a DPP candidate for the Legislative Yuan in Tainan, and several attacks on campaign staff members in various locations around the island. Although gangsters were apparently involved in most of these incidents, the extent to which the attacks were political in nature was difficult to determine. Nonetheless, as a result of the threat of violence, the government ordered the National Security Bureau to protect candidates during the campaign.

The Clean Election Coalition made public a report that listed prices for votes in various districts. According to the report, in Taipei a vote for the Legislative Yuan or city council could be purchased for NT$1,000; a vote for the Taipei County magistrate cost NT$2,000; a vote for representatives from the Fishermen's Association cost NT$3,000; and three votes in Chiayi City cost NT$5,000. Other prices for vote buying were smaller, ranging from NT$200 for a Legislative Yuan vote in Taoyuan County to NT$800 for a vote in Keelung. These rates were not independently verified, but everyone interviewed acknowledged the practice of vote buying. Interestingly, few people thought the purchased votes would make any difference in the election outcome.

The AEI team actually observed few major election irregularities, although reports of various violations were frequently heard. The Taipei Election Commission reported eighty-nine violations as of December 1, the day before the elections.

The most common violations of the Election Law were the illegal placing and size of campaign posters and the setting off of firecrackers.

Many candidates—KMT, DPP, independents, and others—handed out small gifts to supporters. A number of wealthier candidates invited large numbers of potential supporters to expensive banquets. Gifts and banquets are a way of life on Taiwan, however, and it was difficult to draw the line between vote buying and legitimate campaign behavior.

Another irregularity observed was the holding of a private campaign rally while an officially sponsored public rally was going on. At the same public rally, one candidate exceeded her allotted time and refused to step down until she had talked for an additional ten minutes.

One irregularity observed in Taichung was a forged letter from the head of the local retired servicemen's organization criticizing a candidate. In reality, this candidate had received a great deal of support from the retired servicemen. Apparently, the letter was disinformation to discredit the KMT candidate and divide her vote.

Election Results

Over 75 percent of Taiwan's 12 million eligible voters cast ballots on

December 2 in an election that was, for the most part, well managed and orderly.

In a result called an "upset" by KMT Secretary-General James Soong, the ruling party won only 60 percent of the vote, lower than its anticipated 70 percent but still nearly twice the 31 percent of the vote won by the DPP. Independents won most of the remaining 9 percent. In total seats won, the KMT took 70 percent, and the DPP won 22 percent. Independent candidates won most of the remaining 8 percent of the seats. Parties other than the KMT and the DPP fared poorly.

The results of the elections are usefully compared with the elections in 1985 and 1986 (see tables 3–3, 3–4, 3–5, 3–6, and 3–7). In the 1986 Legislative Yuan election, a hundred seats were to be filled. The KMT won seventy-nine; the DPP, running for the first time, won twelve seats. The Young China party won two seats, the China Democratic Socialist party won one seat, and independents won six seats.

In the 1989 elections for the Legislative Yuan 101 seats were contested. The KMT won 72 seats; the DPP won 21; the Young China party and the China Democratic Socialist party won no seats; two of the larger new parties, the Labor party and the Worker's party, won no seats; and independents won 8 seats.

Hence, in the Legislative Yuan, the KMT, while still by far the dominant party, lost about 10 percent of its previously elected seats, while the DPP increased its percentage of seats by about 73 percent. To keep this in perspective, however, we should note that the KMT won fifty more seats than the DPP, more than twice the total number of seats won by the DPP. Considering only the seats available in the election, the KMT maintained a 3.4 to 1 edge over the DPP in the Legislative Yuan. Independents maintained approximately the same number of seats previously won, roughly 8 percent of the total seats open for election.

Of the hundred and one newly elected parliamentarians, seventy-nine were chosen directly by the general population, eighteen were chosen by vocational groups, and four were chosen by the aborigine population. Of the seventy-nine generally elected seats, the KMT won fifty-five, the DPP won eighteen, and independents won six. In the vocational elections, the KMT won thirteen, the DPP won three, and independents won two. The KMT won all four seats reserved for aborigine representatives.

Of the seventy-two KMT winners, fifty-six were official party nominees. Of the twenty-one DPP winners, twenty were official party nominees. Eighteen of the winning KMT candidates were second-generation mainlanders, all of whom favored a reunited China and

47

Taiwan. On the opposite side of this issue were eight new DPP members of the New Nation Alliance favoring an independent Taiwan.

Of those winning in the Legislative Yuan race, eighty-eight were men and thirteen were women. Their average age was forty-five. Their educational background was high: ten had doctorates, twenty-six had master's degrees, fifty-three had bachelor's degrees, and twelve had a senior high school education.

TABLE 3–3

PARTY REPRESENTATION IN THE LEGISLATIVE YUAN
AFTER THE ELECTIONS OF 1986 AND 1989

	1986		1989	
	Number of seats	Percentage	Number of seats	Percentage
KMT	79	79	72	71.28
DPP	12	12	21	20.80
Young China party	2	2	0	0
China Democratic Socialist party	1	1	0	0
Labor party[a]	0	0	0	0
Worker's party[a]	0	0	0	0
Others	6	6	8	7.92
Total seats available	100	100	101	100

a. Not legal in the 1986 elections.
SOURCE: Author.

As for provincial affiliation, seventy-six were from Taiwan Province, one from Taipei City, six from Kaohsiung City, three from Fujian Province, three from Hunan Province, three from Zhejiang Province, two from Shandong Province, two from Henan Province, one from Hubei Province, one from Shanghai City, one from Shanxi Province, one from Jiangsu Province, and one from Nunkiang (a province in Manchuria).

An interesting comparison also emerges in an examination of the results of the 1985 and the 1989 elections for the Taiwan Provincial Assembly. In both elections seventy-seven seats were available. In 1985 the KMT won fifty-nine seats, or 77 percent; the Young China party won one seat; and independents, then called *tangwai*, won seventeen, or 22 percent. The DPP was not formed until the following year.

In the 1989 election the KMT won fifty-four Provincial Assembly seats, or 70 percent; the DPP won sixteen, or 21 percent; the Young

China party, the China Democratic Socialist party, the Labor party, and the Worker's party won no seats; and other parties and independents won seven seats, or 9 percent.

This meant that in the 1989 elections, the KMT lost about 8 percent of its previous seats, while the DPP jumped from no representatives in the Provincial Assembly to one in every five members. Nonetheless, the KMT still retained an overwhelming 3.3 to 1 advantage over the DPP. Significantly, independents and other parties lost 61 percent of their representatives. Many independents, however, no doubt shifted their allegiance to the DPP during the 1985–1989 period. The large fall in the number of independents and the lack of winners among other parties suggest that at the provincial level a two-party system is emerging between the KMT and the DPP (see table 3–4).

A similar trend toward bipolarity appeared in the Taipei City Council race (see table 3–5). In the 1985 and the 1989 Taipei City Council elections, fifty-one seats were available. In 1985 the KMT won thirty-eight seats, or 75 percent; and independents won thirteen seats, or 25 percent. The DPP was not yet formed.

In the 1989 elections, the KMT won thirty-six, or 71 percent; the DPP won fourteen, or 27 percent; and others won one seat, or 2 percent. The KMT thus lost about 5 percent of its seats on the Taipei City Council, while the DPP won about one in every four seats. The KMT maintained a healthy 2.6 to 1 advantage over the DPP in seats won. Other parties and independents won only one seat, again suggesting that most *tangwai* supporters had probably shifted to the DPP by 1989.

In the 1985 elections for the Kaohsiung City Council, the KMT won thirty-two of the forty-two available seats, or 76 percent. Independents won ten seats, or 24 percent. In 1989, the KMT won twenty-nine of forty-three seats, or 67 percent; the DPP won eight seats, or 19 percent; the Labor party won one seat; and others won five seats, or 12 percent.

In the Kaohsiung City Council race, then, the KMT lost 11.5 percent of its seats, while the DPP picked up about one out of every five seats. The KMT still held a large 3.6 to 1 edge in seats over the DPP, however. Other parties and independents seem about equal in strength to the DPP in Kaohsiung, winning a total of six seats, or 14 percent. In Kaohsiung, therefore, the trend toward bipolarity is not as pronounced as in other areas of Taiwan, perhaps because of the strength of local factions and political families. Still, independent candidates seem to have lost about half their supporters to the DPP since the 1985 election.

The elections for county magistrates and city mayors attracted a great deal of attention, since this forum was the focus of DPP strategy. In

49

TABLE 3–4
PARTY REPRESENTATION IN THE PROVINCIAL ASSEMBLY
AFTER THE ELECTIONS OF 1985 AND 1989

	1985		1989	
	Number of seats	Percentage	Number of seats	Percentage
KMT	59	76.62	54	70.12
DPP[a]	0	0	16	20.78
Young China party	1	1.30	0	0
China Democratic Socialist party	0	0	0	0
Labor party[a]	0	0	0	0
Worker's party[a]	0	0	0	0
Others	17	22.08	7	9.10
Total seats available	77	100	77	100

a. Not legal in the 1985 elections.
SOURCE: Author.

both the 1985 and the 1989 elections, twenty-one seats were available for sixteen county magistrates and five city mayors. Each local official serves a four-year term.

In the 1985 local elections, the KMT won seventeen seats, or 81 percent, while independents won four seats, or 19 percent. In 1989 the KMT won fourteen of the seats, or 67 percent; the DPP won six seats, or 29 percent; and independents won one seat.

Of the sixteen county magistrate seats, the KMT won fourteen seats in the 1985 elections, or 87.5 percent; and independents won two seats, or 12.5 percent. In 1989 the KMT won ten magistrate seats, or 62.5 percent; and the DPP won six seats, or 37.5 percent. No other parties or independents won county magistrate seats. Local elections gave the DPP its highest level of success, demonstrating that its strategy was effective in targeting local executive positions.

The KMT won four seats of the five mayoral seats in 1985, or 80 percent, while independents won one seat. In the 1989 elections, the KMT also won four out of five seats, and independents again won the other seat.

In the local elections as a whole, the KMT lost 18 percent of its seats, while the DPP won nearly one-third of the seats. Since only one

TABLE 3–5
PARTY REPRESENTATION IN THE TAIPEI CITY COUNCIL
AFTER THE ELECTIONS OF 1985 AND 1989

	1985		1989	
	Number of seats	Percentage	Number of seats	Percentage
KMT	38	74.51	36	70.59
DPP[a]	0	0	14	27.45
Young China party	0	0	0	0
China Democratic Socialist party	0	0	0	0
Labor party[a]	0	0	0	0
Worker's party[a]	0	0	0	0
Others	13	25.49	1	1.96
Total seats available	51	100	51	100

a. Not legal in the 1985 elections.
SOURCE: Author.

independent won a local seat (for Chiayi City mayor), it appears that bipolarity will exist between the KMT and the DPP at the local level as well. The Chiayi City mayor announced soon after the elections that she would join the DPP county magistrates in an alliance to press the national government for greater local autonomy.

Again, it should be kept in mind that of the twenty-one total local seats, the KMT won more than twice as many seats as the DPP, maintaining a 2.3 to 1 advantage. The DPP, however, gained tremendous political power by winning six of sixteen county magistrate positions. In local politics, the DPP now governs roughly half the territory of Taiwan and 35 percent of its population. Those counties won by the DPP were Hsinchu, Changhua, Ilan, Kaohsiung, Pingtung, and, most important, Taipei. Taipei County is the island's most important political center, the home of ROC President Lee Teng-hui, and an area the KMT believed it could not afford to lose.

A total of 293 seats were up for election in 1989. The KMT won 205 of these, or 70 percent. Since it had 346 candidates out of the total number of 722 candidates, or 48 percent, the KMT's success ratio (number of victors per total number of KMT candidates) was 59 percent In other words, three out of every five KMT candidates won office. This

TABLE 3–6

PARTY REPRESENTATION IN THE KAOHSIUNG CITY COUNCIL
AFTER THE ELECTIONS OF 1985 AND 1989

	1985		1989	
	Number of seats	Percentage	Number of seats	Percentage
KMT	32	76.20	29	67.44
DPP[a]	0	0	8	18.60
Young China party	0	0	0	0
China Democratic Socialist party	0	0	0	0
Labor party[a]	0	0	1	2.33
Worker's party[a]	0	0	0	0
Others	10	23.80	5	11.63
Total seats available	42	100	43	100

a. Not legal in the 1985 elections.
SOURCE: Author.

compares very favorably with the DPP and other contending parties and independents.

The DPP had a total of 163 candidates and won sixty-five seats, or 22 percent of the total available seats. The DPP enjoyed a 40 percent success rate; two out of every five of its candidates won. The ratio of total KMT winners to total DPP winners was 3.15 to 1, whereas the ratio of the total KMT candidates to total DPP candidates was 2.12 to 1. Although its performance was less favorable than that of the KMT, the DPP proved itself a very credible, though still small, opposition party to the KMT.

The Young China party had a total of four candidates and won no seats. The China Democratic Socialist party ran five candidates and won no seats. The newly formed Worker's party ran four candidates and won no seats. The new Labor party ran fifteen candidates and won one seat, or a 7 percent success ratio. Other parties and independents ran 185 candidates and won twenty-two seats, for a 12 percent success ratio.

Since the Legislative Yuan races were rather unusual in that representatives from both functional (twenty-two seats) and geographic districts (seventy-nine seats) were elected, it is interesting to factor out that election and concentrate on the Provincial Assembly, Taipei City

TABLE 3–7
PARTY AFFILIATION OF MAGISTRATES AND MAYORS
AFTER THE ELECTIONS OF 1985 AND 1989

	1985		1989	
	Number of seats	Percentage	Number of seats	Percentage
KMT	17	80.95	14	66.67
DPP[a]	0	0	6	28.57
Young China party	0	0	0	0
China Democratic Socialist party	0	0	0	0
Labor party[a]	0	0	0	0
Worker's party[a]	0	0	0	0
Others	4	19.05	1	4.76
Total seats available	21	100	21	100

a. Not legal in the 1985 elections.
SOURCE: Author.

Council, Kaohsiung City Council, and county magistrate and mayoral elections. In these elections, voters had an opportunity to determine the total membership of the elected bodies and administrative offices. Moreover, since these local officials play a more substantive role in the lives of the average voter on Taiwan, the results of these elections should provide a fair indication of the relative local strength of the KMT, the DPP, and other parties and independents.

Altogether, 420 candidates sought 192 seats in these local elections. KMT candidates totaled 206, and KMT winners totaled 133. Thus, the KMT won 69 percent of the local seats, while it ran 49 percent of the candidates. Its success ratio was a very respectable 65 percent.

The DPP ran 106 candidates and won forty-four seats, thus winning 23 percent of the seats with 30 percent of the candidates. The DPP success ratio was 41.5 percent. The Labor party won one seat in the local elections with 7 candidates, for a 14 percent success rate. Other parties and independents (not including the Young China party, the China Democratic Socialist party, and the Worker's party, which had a total of five local candidates but did not win any seats) had a total of 96 candidates and won fourteen seats. This represented 23 percent of the total local candidates and 7 percent of the total local winners. The success ratio for other parties and independents was thus about 15 percent.

Since results from the local elections are roughly equal to the results from all the elections, including the Legislative Yuan, a fair conclusion is that the 1989 elections demonstrated that the KMT continues to enjoy strong support throughout Taiwan, but that the DPP is a worthy competitor. Other parties and independents had limited success in the elections and may become even less significant in the future if the DPP is able to draw away more of their supporters through successful policies in areas under its administration.

4

Analysis and Policy Implications

Taiwan is a classic example of a country making the difficult transition from an authoritarian regime to a democracy. All the elements of hope and danger that such a transition entails can be found in modern Taiwan, along with numerous conditions uniquely Chinese.

One of the principal problems confronting Taiwan is that democratization occurred without adequate legal and procedural mechanisms in place. Within a remarkably short time, President Chiang Ching-kuo lifted martial law, permitted the formation of opposition political parties, removed restrictions on some forms of contact with mainland China, and instituted reforms within the KMT and the ROC government.

Just as Taiwan needed major infrastructure improvements to "take off" economically, so Taiwan needs a legal and political framework to develop politically if democracy is to work efficiently. In many respects, the bureaucrats still have not caught up with the scope of Chiang's reforms and subsequent events.

Slowing the administrative adjustment further is the new relationship between the ruling party and the government. In the past, the KMT would use ROC government officials to do its will. Now, by deliberately separating the functions of party and government, the KMT can only provide guidance and rely on persuasion to move government officials in a particular direction.

Another major change is that the KMT must now fight for its power. The KMT's right to rule is challenged not only by the DPP but also by a host of other parties and special interest groups. Many of these opposition groups attempt to influence government policy through confrontation.

Without question, the wild cards in Taiwan's politics are the DPP and the other opposition parties. If these opposition groups decide to become a "loyal opposition" and pursue their interests through legitimate channels, then democracy will flourish on Taiwan. If, however, the DPP or other opposition parties try to undermine Taiwan's political system as a short-cut to power, then a return to martial law or military intervention by the PRC is a scenario that cannot be ruled out.

Some evidence suggests that the DPP will choose the role of loyal opposition—at least for the time being. Stung by criticism of its antics in the Legislative Yuan in late 1988 and early 1989, the DPP reexamined its tactics during the spring of 1989. Several members interviewed believed the party was alienating Taiwan's large and important middle class, which values stability as a prerequisite to continued economic growth. An increasing number of people expressed the view that the DPP was useful as an opposition party but that it had failed to offer constructive policy alternatives to the KMT. Perhaps as a result of these criticisms, an impressive number of DPP candidates in the December 1989 elections focused on substantive issues such as tax reform, privatization of state-run enterprises, termination of business monopolies, and review of mainland trade policy, rather than more radical agendas.

A fundamental problem remains, however, in that many DPP members seem intent on changing Taiwan's political system, refusing, for example, to accept the ROC name, constitution, or flag. Denying allegiance to a common nation makes cooperation between the KMT and the DPP very difficult.

The DPP has thus had both positive and negative effects on Taiwan's politics. On the positive side, the DPP has provided needed checks and balances in the political process. The DPP has also become a powerful incentive to the KMT to continue reforms and to become more responsive to public opinion. On the negative side, the DPP's tactics of confrontation—if carried too far—may undermine Taiwan's evolving and as yet fragile democracy. On balance, however, the positive effects of the DPP seem to have outweighed the negative.

The rise of the DPP has forced the issue of Taiwan's independence to the surface. Until 1987, promotion of Taiwan's independence was illegal and punishable under martial law. But in that year the DPP held a number of demonstrations in support of "self-determination," a code word often meaning Taiwan's independence. The subsequent public debate, largely critical of the demonstrations, suggested that independence was considered a dangerous idea by the majority of Taiwanese.

That the DPP is able to continue to use Taiwan's independence as a divisive issue, as shown in the 1989 elections, indicates that the idea of independence may be more dormant than dead. This is true despite the disappearing differences between the mainlanders and the Taiwanese through intermarriage, a common educational system, equal opportunities in public service, and over four decades of a common culture.

Observations and Analysis

Discussions with many foreign observers indicate a consensus that the 1989 elections had few major irregularities. The elections were fairer, freer, and more orderly than elections in the past. Most observers concluded that a process of power sharing was under way on Taiwan for the first time, that the people would be given increased power to choose their leaders and national policies in the future, and that the ROC government's respect for civil liberties had improved vastly over previous elections.

There were some criticisms, however. Most observers expressed dissatisfaction over access to the electronic media. By law, no candidate was allowed to campaign on radio or television. But the opposition charged that KMT candidates appeared much more frequently than opposition candidates on television game shows, news, interviews, and other programs.

Since the three television channels on Taiwan are controlled by the KMT, the Taiwan provincial government, and the military, this issue will continue to be controversial until some equitable solution is found. Part of the problem is that all television broadcasts reach the entire island, not just local communities. There is no reason why the citizens of Kaohsiung, for example, should hear campaign speeches from candidates for the Taipei City Council.

Several foreign observers interviewed echoed the DPP's complaints about the fairness of the elections. "Fairness" is difficult to address objectively, since most of the complaints stem from the advantages the KMT enjoys over the DPP by virtue of being the ruling party. Over the years, the KMT has created an enormous organization and has been integrated into virtually every aspect of society. Even if the election process were 100 percent "fair," these KMT advantages would be very difficult for any opposition party to overcome.

Another criticism leveled by many foreign observers was that the Election Commission did not enforce the rules. The root of the problem seemed to be in the Election Law itself, which attempted through regulations to micromanage every aspect of the campaign. This proved to be impossible. According to election officials, violations fell into two main categories: campaign rallies lasting longer than two hours and campaign materials placed outside legal limits. The officials admitted they frequently ignored minor violations.

The commission exercised only administrative powers, not judicial powers. Punishment was generally met by a small fine. Serious judicial violations, such as bribery or violence, were forwarded to the judiciary. According to commission officials, 211 cases of violations of national security law occurred during the elections.

There was a limited amount of postelection violence. The most serious incident occurred in Tainan, where riots broke out over an announced KMT victory in the Tainan County race for magistrate. The rioters seized and damaged a county building. An election recount did not substantiate the DPP candidate's claims, however, and the KMT candidate retained his seat.[27]

Many observers commented that the KMT and the DPP candidates advocated very similar social, economic, and environmental policies on issues such as pollution, crime, traffic, social welfare, labor, taxes, and education. To distinguish themselves, candidates reminded voters of their past accomplishments and promised future service to constituents. In Taichung City and Taichung County, one area observed by the author, almost every candidate argued that senior parliamentarians should resign from the Legislative Yuan and the National Assembly. The candidates universally opposed the ROC's policy prohibiting direct contact with the mainland. All favored direct elections for the ROC president, governor of Taiwan Province, and mayors of Taipei and Kaohsiung. Almost all candidates spoke in Taiwanese, not Mandarin, the official ROC dialect.

In these local elections, tangible issues clearly were more important than intangible ones. Most voters interviewed were concerned about the deterioration of the quality of life on Taiwan since 1986, particularly traffic jams, increased crime, and environmental pollution. This concern hurt the KMT because the ruling party had not solved these problems. In the local elections, the determinants for victory included party affiliation, family ties, personality, stance on local issues, publicity, and campaign spending. Since candidates spent 20–30 percent more for this than for previous elections, the money sent by party headquarters to individual candidates had to be supplemented by contributions from individuals and businesses.

Analysis. Several trends appeared during the elections. First, it was significant that the third largest group of candidates (171 individuals, or 24 percent of those running) did not belong to any party. A large number of independents ran because the KMT and the DPP, as well as other parties, did not meet the needs of a sizable percentage of the population.

58

Although independents were anti-KMT, they did not want to join the DPP. The strength of the independents led to speculation that a third major political party might be formed to compete against the KMT and the DPP. During the elections, however, little evidence indicated that independents agreed on a joint platform. In general, the performance of independents was not outstanding.

A second important trend was that the platforms of both the KMT and the DPP emphasized social policy issues, reflecting the public's growing concern over improving the quality of life on Taiwan. Local politicians focused on issues such as city development, crime, pollution, the environment, and traffic. National issues were not the deciding issues in the 1989 election.

A third trend was the growing involvement of business at all levels of the elections. Caucuses promoting business interests appeared throughout the island. The business groups cut across party lines and backed those candidates who promised to serve business interests once in office. Because of the importance of economic growth to Taiwan, the rise of a strong business interest in politics may eventually prove a better organized and financed challenge to the KMT than that coming from the DPP.

Other trends of note included the changing role of the media in politics. The media, especially print, traditionally reported events and points of view. But in this election the media vocally advocated policy and supported individual candidates. Of interest also was the greater number of mainlanders running in this election. The success of the second-generation mainlanders may suggest that people under the age of forty are not identified as being mainlanders or Taiwanese by most voters. Another interpretation is that mainlanders voted in blocs for their own candidates. As noted previously, the single-vote, multimember electoral system enables an organized minority to elect candidates to the Legislative Yuan, Provincial Assembly, and city councils.

The Parties

The election outcome invites many interpretations. One of the most astute was offered by Parris Chang, a political scientist from Pennsylvania State University. In his assessment, the margin of the KMT defeat was just about right. On the one hand, if the KMT had lost too many seats, the hard-liners within the party might vote against the reformers and slow progress toward democracy. On the other hand, he argued, if the DPP lost too many seats, the opposition might become fully radicalized.[28]

Whether a transition of power will actually occur someday on Taiwan is uncertain at this point, but the 1989 elections did usher in a new era of party politics. While the KMT remained the strongest party and the ruling party, the DPP emerged as a significant opposition capable of winning at least 30 percent of the popular vote and 20–30 percent of available seats, including powerful local executive posts. The election also revealed the strengths and weaknesses of both parties. The KMT, for example, exhibited great organizational and financial strength. Although weak in these areas, the DPP proved capable of fielding many attractive candidates and articulating policies across a broad spectrum of issues that were appealing to voters.

The success of the DPP will prove a major inconvenience to the KMT. If they choose, local DPP officials can refuse to allow the KMT to hold party meetings in government buildings or can make the ruling party pay rent for its meetings in public buildings. DPP officials can put restrictions on the China Youth Corps, take down Chiang Ching-kuo's picture in city office buildings, and make it more difficult for KMT members to receive appointments to prestigious local jobs. As a result of its victories, the DPP will be able to appoint its members to various positions, particularly in the territory under opposition control. This will tend to diffuse political membership in social organizations throughout the island.

As the KMT separates party functions from those of the government, politics on Taiwan will become more equal. A more "level playing field," in turn, might result in more DPP winners in future elections—assuming, of course, that the DPP does not self-destruct through fragmentation or through the adoption of unpopular, radical policies. All in all, these developments are good for the growth of democracy on Taiwan and contribute to the creation of a more pluralistic society. But the process of change will force the KMT, and the DPP to some extent, to make far-reaching and painful choices about its future role in Taiwan politics.

The Kuomintang. First among these choices for the KMT will be a redefinition of the role of the party. Is the KMT a revolutionary party, a democratic party, or both? To what extent should the KMT lead the people, and to what extent should it be led by the people?

The historical mission of the KMT requires it to be a revolutionary party dedicated to the liberation of mainland China and a democratic party reflecting the will of the people. But who are "the people" in this instance? Are they the people of all of China, in which case the KMT cannot allow itself to be governed by democracy on Taiwan, if that leads to Taiwan's independence; or are they the people of Taiwan, in which case the KMT may have to forgo its role of leading all China toward an eventual democracy?

KMT leaders believe the party has a dual character as both a revolutionary and a democratic party and a dual responsibility for both leading public opinion and following public opinion. But this is more easily said than done. To accomplish this dual role in an era of democracy on Taiwan, the KMT will have to persuade the people of Taiwan that it is in their interests to pursue these twin objectives. The people of Taiwan will have to be convinced to accept the need of the government not only to solve immediate problems but also to pursue a long-term policy of seeking China's reunification under a democratic regime.

Persuading the Taiwanese people that such is the case may not be an easy task, especially when one considers that the KMT has had nearly forty years of control over the media and educational systems to inculcate that idea. If it has not yet taken hold, then optimism about the KMT's ability to convince the people of Taiwan now may not be justified.

As evidenced by statements of concern about a KMT "upset" in the elections, KMT leaders may have panicked a bit as the returns became known.[29] Interviews disclosed two possible explanations for this response. One was that the election returns, particularly for county magistrates, sent a danger signal that the KMT organization was breaking down at the grass-roots level. Since the central government and the provincial government on Taiwan overlap nearly 100 percent, the KMT's loss of local control might well lead to loss of central control.

The second explanation was that moderate KMT leaders overemphasized the loss to give a "democratic feeling" to the election outcome. Under this interpretation, moderate leaders wanted to use the KMT setback to cast blame on the conservatives within the party as a way to force them out of positions of power.

KMT reformers now face the headache of how to convince senior parliamentarians to retire in the very near future. Those holding office since 1947 proved to be a great embarrassment to KMT candidates in the elections, many of whom denounced the senior leaders in their campaign speeches. The reformers must handle the senior parliamentarians very carefully, however, because they control the National Assembly. If offended, they could elect someone other than Lee Teng-hui for president.[30]

In introducing democracy on Taiwan, the KMT has risked the preservation of its own power. The KMT's structure has weakened significantly in recent years, as shown by the many KMT candidates in the last election who severely criticized their own party. Still, many KMT leaders

61

believe the ROC must remain under a form of political tutelage. The ruling party, they hold, should direct the evolution of democracy from the
top down, much as it directed the stages of Taiwan's economic development. The practical effect of this view is that the KMT must continue to
maintain control of the island.

This creates a basic dilemma. From the ruling party's perspective,
the elections were a step in a continuum of progressive movement toward
full democracy. Although the ruling party has strong institutional advantages that most members do not want to give up, they recognize that the
KMT must reform if it is to appeal to voters. The election results may be
a sign that the ruling party is not reforming fast enough.

Thoughtful KMT leaders must ask themselves whether it is possible
for any ruling party, after forty years of unchallenged power, to democratize and still preserve its leading role through free elections. As seen in
the case of several Eastern European countries, people will often vote the
ruling party out of office because they want to give someone else a
chance. Whether this will be the case on Taiwan remains to be seen.

The Democratic Progressive Party. Not surprisingly, the DPP takes
a view of the evolution of Taiwan's democracy different from that of the
KMT. As its political platform shows, the DPP wants democracy to evolve
without continued KMT tutelage. The DPP approach means the dis-
mantling of the KMT's structures throughout society.

Just as the KMT must redefine itself as a result of the political
transformation now under way on Taiwan, so the DPP must determine
what type of opposition party it should become. If the DPP is serious
about ruling Taiwan through democratic elections, then it must act
responsibly and appeal to mainstream voters. Since the KMT remains the
ruling party, the DPP must cooperate with the KMT to solve the many
immediate problems now facing the nation.

Many in the DPP view this as a practical step to ensure the party's
future. A substantial number of DPP members, however, are much more
radical in their approach to power, preferring to disrupt the functions of
the existing government and to promote policies to effect immediate
change in the country's direction. Taiwan's independence is sometimes
advocated by these individuals.

The DPP received between 30 and 35 percent of the popular vote.
An accurate count is difficult, because many independents were closely
associated with the DPP. Since DPP membership was about 20,000,
many individuals voted for the opposition party without actually belong-
ing to it. According to the statements and opinions of numerous voters

interviewed on Taiwan after the elections, their motivations for voting DPP were diverse.

Some DPP candidates, like You Ching, winner of the key Taipei County magistrate's seat, were voted into office through a hard-fought campaign against a worthy opponent. Some DPP candidates were said to receive large numbers of sympathy votes. Other voters decided to cast ballots against the KMT because they liked individual opposition candidates more than the KMT competition. Other voters believed the KMT had too much power and decided to vote for DPP candidates to dilute that power somewhat.

Many of those interviewed said they voted for the DPP because they were dissatisfied with the KMT's performance in recent years, especially its failure to solve the problems of pollution, traffic, and crime. Often these voters said they knew that the DPP would probably do no better but that since the KMT had ruled for forty years, someone else should have a chance to solve the problems. Still others voted for the DPP because they believed Taiwan had reached a stage of development where it should have its own government, not a government controlled by mainlanders.

Thus most individuals probably voted for the DPP not because of party affiliation, but because of myriad other factors. If the DPP is to become a permanent fixture in Taiwan politics, it must find a way to draw these circumstantial supporters into a stronger commitment to the DPP. Otherwise, the KMT may be able to attract their votes in future elections.

Politics

Following the elections, DPP leaders outlined various priorities. These included removing the KMT from school and college campuses, implementing a national health insurance program, gaining more local autonomy in education, accelerating the privatization of state-owned enterprises, maintaining closer scrutiny of the defense budget, and gaining control of city and county budgets and policies. DPP leaders also said they wanted to review licensing procedures for television stations.

The nature of these priorities suggests that competition between the KMT and the DPP will intensify as the DPP begins to exercise real power. This competition is more complex than that between two similar parties such as the Democratic and the Republican parties in the United States. The two parties on Taiwan hold diametrically opposed views about what constitutes the nation of Taiwan, how power should be distributed on the island, what priorities should govern policy, and what Taiwan's future relationship should be with the mainland.

To sustain its political initiative, the KMT promises further reforms in the near future. Areas of political reform include revision of the Temporary Provisions, the direct election of the mayors of Taipei and Kaohsiung, and the direct election of the majority of members in the National Assembly. Direct election for the ROC president was not possible, some KMT officials contended, because it would not be appropriate for the ROC president to be elected by the people of only one province of China.

Party leaders interviewed stressed that the KMT is sincere in wanting Taiwan to develop into a meaningful democracy and that this requires effective opposition parties. These officials say that the ruling party feels responsible for creating an environment in which such opposition parties can grow. But because democracy by its very nature moves in unprescribed ways, it may not evolve in a direction desired by the KMT.

Many DPP members, for example, do not support the present ROC government. At least one major faction of the DPP wants a revolutionary change of government on Taiwan. Thus, a large percentage of DPP members are not loyal citizens of the ROC: they are loyal to Taiwan. To the KMT, advocating an independent Taiwan is not a public policy debate but an expression of disloyalty to the nation.

The divisive issue of whether to seek eventual reunification or Taiwan's independence will remain at the core of Taiwan's politics. If problems persist in Taiwan's transition to democracy, they will be due largely to the difficulty of finding a workable compromise between the KMT, which is historically committed to working toward a united, democratic China, and an opposition party seeking to serve Taiwan's—not mainland China's—interests.

The attitude of many Taiwanese interviewed, who were not DPP members, was this: "For forty years the people of Taiwan have been taught about the godlike qualities of Sun Yat-sen, Chiang Kai-shek, Chiang Ching-kuo, and the KMT. In many ways, the Taiwanese were made to feel like second-class citizens. Now, the Taiwanese have a chance to rule the island, and they intend to do so. The KMT's success in leading Taiwan for the past forty years does not give it the right to retain power now. The democratization of Taiwan's political system is not merely a policy direction initiated by the KMT. Democracy has also resulted from the evolution of social awareness on the island, from economic stability and prosperity, from mass education, and from access to the outside world. To compete fairly for power with other contending parties and groups, the KMT must change its structure and character."

These demands for rapid change in Taiwan's politics place great

64

strain on the KMT. It is difficult for senior Nationalist officials to give up their vested interests in the power structure of the past. That the KMT has been willing to reform itself is remarkable; that it will be able to maintain power after reforming may be even more remarkable.

A certain unfairness underlies this process. A common view encountered on Taiwan was that the KMT is not doing well in solving problems such as pollution and the declining quality of life. But these complaints often overlooked the fact that these problems have resulted largely from the KMT's huge success in developing the island's economy since the 1950s.

One serious problem may be that the KMT is not reforming fast enough. Social frustration and economic problems are building up rapidly. Taiwan, for example, is losing its competitive edge in world markets. Labor costs on Taiwan have increased to the point where many factories are moving to neighboring countries, taking advanced technology with them. It is the role of the government to solve this type of problem; yet many believe that the KMT and the ROC government lack decisiveness on this and other crucial issues.

Relations with the PRC

A critical variable in Taiwan's future is the PRC. Surprisingly, the events of Tiananmen Square in June 1989 do not seem to have had an important impact on the December elections. Had the elections been held within a few weeks of the June massacre, the KMT would probably have benefited. At minimum, the people of Taiwan would have admitted that the ruling party had been right about the brutal nature of Communist rule. As it turned out, the Tiananmen incident and subsequent PRC threats against Taiwan may have actually benefited the DPP. Some Taiwanese said their votes for the opposition party reflected their rejection of the PRC as having a role in Taiwan's affairs.

A democratic Taiwan presents major problems for Beijing, particularly if the issue of Taiwan's independence looms in importance to voters. Public discussion of the issue in the 1989 elections was a marked change from previous years. Democracy on Taiwan is not necessarily equivalent to Taiwan independence. The emergence of independence as an issue to be decided in a democratic setting, however, means that the people of Taiwan want to determine their own national identity. This prospect frightens the PRC and many Nationalist Chinese on Taiwan.

Beijing has said repeatedly it will use force against Taiwan if the island declares independence. ROC military analysts agree with their

PRC counterparts that China has the capability to invade Taiwan but that the cost would be enormous. More important, these Chinese analysts say that Beijing lacks the political reason to attack Taiwan under current conditions. As part of Taiwan's deterrent strategy, the KMT and the ROC government send very clear signals to the PRC that they will not allow Taiwan to become independent.

One of Chiang Ching-kuo's most important contributions to the democratic process on Taiwan was the removal of the military from a central role in governing Taiwan. But there is a potential difficulty: whereas the military is loyal to the Republic of China and to the ideals of the Nationalist cause, it might not be loyal to the DPP if the DPP intended to declare Taiwan independent.

This point was emphasized by ROC Defense Minister (now premier) Hau Pei-tsun in an appearance before the Legislative Yuan after the December elections. General Hau said, "The ROC military will not defend Taiwan in the case of independence. The ROC military will only defend the Republic of China and the ROC Constitution."[31]

Taiwan's top military leaders view independence as a threat to national security. Some believe the independence movement is currently a greater threat to Taiwan than the PRC. Taiwan's independence is perceived as dangerous not only because the potential for a military confrontation with the PRC is always present, but also because the issue would rend the delicate political fabric of Taiwan. Given the challenges to its survival in the international community, Taiwan would be severely weakened if one segment of the population actively supported Taiwan's independence and another segment vehemently opposed it.

Although most of the candidates in the December elections did not make Taiwan's independence an issue in their campaigns, it hovered importantly in the background. Over this issue, the KMT and DPP are at serious odds. Indeed, the potential exists for a major confrontation on Taiwan over independence.

Such a possibility becomes clear when the KMT and the DPP platforms are compared. To a remarkable degree, the two parties agree on many other policy issues. Both parties, for example, are strongly in favor of continued reform, although the DPP favors a faster pace than the KMT. Both parties favor reducing crime, pollution, and traffic. But on the crucial issue of self-determination—whether the people of Taiwan have a right to separate from the rest of China, if they so choose—the KMT and the DPP are at odds.

To the KMT, reunification of Taiwan with the mainland is a national goal. In explaining this position, KMT leaders often point out that

Taiwanese are ethnically Chinese and cannot leave the mainland as a separate country. As a practical matter, Taiwan is too close to the mainland to be independent. Talk of Taiwan's independence irritates the PRC. The KMT argues that reunification is supported by the great majority of ROC citizens. As many as 90 percent of the people on Taiwan, the ruling party claims, want eventual reunification under the Taiwan Experience. Less than 5 percent of the population favor an independent Republic of Taiwan, although, the ruling party admits, few people actually support immediate or even near-term reunification.

DPP spokesmen, in contrast, frequently argue that the independence of Taiwan has become an issue because the KMT rules Taiwan and because the people do not want to be part of the PRC. The DPP points out that both the KMT and the Chinese Communist party are controlled by mainlanders; inevitably, these parties will pursue policies that promote mainland interests over the interests of Taiwan. At a minimum, the DPP wants a public discussion of this issue and then the opportunity for the people of Taiwan themselves to decide the future of Taiwan and its relationship with the mainland.

The issue of Taiwan's independence, therefore, is emerging as an important and divisive factor in island politics. It was apparent in the elections that the future of Taiwan—whether independence, reunification, or an indefinite prolongation of the status quo—was on people's minds. Yet because it was also apparent to most people that the issue could not be decided in the December elections, the issue played a relatively minor role in the campaign.

The KMT presents a vision of Taiwan as part of a united, democratic China. Many DPP members want an independent Taiwan because the possibility of a democratic China is small and because Taiwanese do not want to be controlled by anyone in Beijing, whether KMT or the Communists. Both parties generally agree, however, that Taiwan's future cannot be solved now. They also generally agree that the main efforts of the government should focus on improving the quality of life on Taiwan and guaranteeing the security of territories currently under the control of the ROC government.

Despite the fact that some KMT and DPP candidates were elected on platforms that included a commitment to reunification or independence, the complexities of defining the future relationship of Taiwan with the mainland suggest that resolving the issue may be lengthy. Given the vast differences between the life styles of the two Chinese societies bordering the Taiwan Strait, it may be in Taipei's and Beijing's self-interests to view the issue from a long-range perspective. Taiwan, for example, needs time to strengthen itself and to encourage reform on the mainland. The PRC needs time to develop its economy and attract Taiwan, as it is said, "like iron to a magnet."

Policy Implications for the United States

The future of Taiwan is uncertain. But what can be said with some degree of confidence is that the DPP's success in the elections and the emergence of Taiwan's independence as a public policy issue are potentially disruptive factors in both ROC-PRC relations and in U.S. relations with both Chinese governments.

Among the many foreign delegations observing Taiwan's elections was a U.S. delegation led by Democratic Congressman Stephen Solarz from New York, chairman of the Asian and Pacific Affairs Subcommittee of the House Foreign Affairs Committee. Congressman Solarz and his colleagues concluded: "Our key judgment is that this year's election was the most free and fair in Taiwan's history."[32] The delegation went on to comment, however, that it could not "say that by any objective standard they were fully free and fully fair." Those areas that the delegation believed prevented the election from being fully free and fully fair were:

- the difficulties opposition candidates faced in gaining access to the electronic media compared with candidates from the ruling party
- restrictions on the discussion of certain subjects like Taiwan's independence
- the disqualification of certain candidates because of their prior conviction under martial law provisions
- the fact that the elections did not offer the opportunity of reallocating power

The final point was most important to the congressional delegation, because legitimate elections in the American sense have the potential of redistributing power to different parties and individuals. Such a shift in power could not take place in the Legislative Yuan in the 1989 elections (because the number of seats available for election was limited), although elections for the Provincial Assembly, Taipei and Kaohsiung city councils, and county magistrates and city mayors did meet this criterion.

The congressional visit was the latest in a series of U.S. government efforts to encourage the development of democracy on Taiwan. Believing that opposition politics are an essential element of democracy, several influential senators and congressmen openly support the *tangwai* and the DPP. Whereas this is understandable in the American political context,

U.S. support for the democratization of Taiwan has led some DPP members to assume that the United States would support an independent Taiwan.

The probability of U.S. support for Taiwan's independence is small, given the likely adverse effect this would have on relations between the United States and the PRC, but that support should not be dismissed entirely. Possible U.S. support would depend primarily on circumstances. Whether to support Taiwan's independence could become a heated public debate in the United States. Given the historical vacillation of U.S. policy toward China, it would be a mistake to reject the possibility that the United States would support an independent Taiwan.

Since the 1989 election brought the issue to the surface, U.S. policy toward Taiwan's independence should be examined in more detail. A fundamental principle of U.S. policy toward China since the late 1960s has been that the Chinese people themselves should resolve the issue of Taiwan in a peaceful manner.[33] This principle is found in the main documents governing Sino-American relations, including the 1972 Shanghai Communiqué, the December 1978 U.S. statement accompanying the U.S.-PRC Joint Communiqué on the Establishment of Diplomatic Relations, the 1979 Taiwan Relations Act, and the U.S. statement accompanying the August 17, 1982, U.S.-PRC Joint Communiqué.

These documents also contain another important statement of U.S. policy: the acknowledgment that both Taipei and Beijing insist there is only one China and that Taiwan is part of China. "Acknowledgment" is a carefully chosen word. It does not equate to "acceptance" of the Chinese position, although the United States does not "challenge" the Chinese view. There is deliberate ambiguity here.

According to some analysts on Taiwan, it may not be in Taiwan's interests for the United States to declare openly its support for an independent Taiwan. In the first place, these analysts argue, the PRC is not afraid of the United States, because Washington is not perceived as having sufficient political will to use its military might against China. Admittedly, some in Beijing are concerned that the United States might support Taiwan's independence if the PRC uses force, but the predominant PRC assessment, according to these analysts, is that the United States would probably not support Taiwan if China presented the United States with a *fait accompli*.

Second, the analysts say, many on Taiwan do not think the United States will immediately use force to help Taiwan. The issue would be debated in the administration and in Congress. If Taiwan could hold out, then the probability increases that the United States would come to Taiwan's aid with military equipment at least. But the burden of defense

69

will rest on Taiwan's shoulders, not those of the United States. Third, U.S. policy can change quickly and unexpectedly. There is no guarantee that U.S. support would forever be forthcoming to an independent Taiwan, even if one president or Congress had supported Taiwan's independence at some earlier date.

Fourth, the United States is not well positioned militarily to prevent a determined PRC assault against Taiwan. If current plans for a reduction of U.S. military forces in the Asia-Pacific region go forward, then the capacity of the United States to intervene militarily on Taiwan's behalf diminishes even further. Fifth, if the United States openly declared its support for Taiwan's independence, Beijing might speed up preparations for an assault against the island. The one-China principle is a fundamental dogma with Beijing. If the United States pushes the PRC too far on this issue, it would cause problems for Taiwan.

Given these factors, the analysts conclude, the United States should remain ambiguous on Taiwan's independence. On an issue of this sensitivity, the United States should not be too clear. If the issue is clarified, then it will harm everyone's interests, particularly Taiwan's.

Whatever the merits of this argument, the very sensitivity of the issue makes it clear that U.S. interests are best served by a continuation of the status quo in the Taiwan Strait. Officially, the United States supports a peaceful resolution without prejudice as to whether Taiwan will be independent or reunited with mainland China.[34] What matters to Washington is that the process of resolution be peaceful and supported by both Chinese governments. As the 1989 elections demonstrated, however, the role of the people on Taiwan in this process is a consideration that will probably grow in the future as Taiwan becomes more democratic.

The difficulty the United States faces is that the processes now under way on Taiwan and on the mainland may not ultimately favor a peaceful resolution. On Taiwan, for example, the forces of independence are becoming more visible, if not necessarily stronger. Those on Taiwan dedicated to eventual reunification with the mainland seem to be more isolated and fewer in number. On mainland China, the forces of conservatism are becoming stronger, although for how long is difficult to determine. Those on the mainland favoring the creation of conditions necessary to attract Taiwan are no longer in power. Thus, current trends on both sides of the Taiwan Strait seem to be away from, not toward, a peaceful resolution of the Taiwan issue based on mutual accommodation and mutual benefit.

But current trends may not necessarily be the dominant ones. Seen from a perspective of fifty years, far more peaceful interaction now occurs

70

between the two Chinese sides than ever before. There is also wider recognition that a nonpeaceful resolution of the issue would be against the interests of both sides. Furthermore, reduced U.S. intervention in the Taiwan issue allows the Chinese to reach their own settlement without undue foreign pressure. Conditions on mainland China are far better now than in previous decades, although conditions have deteriorated economically over the past two years and politically since Tiananmen Square. The long-term trends, therefore, seem to favor an eventual solution that is peaceful and perhaps in the interests of both China and Taiwan. Under most circumstances, such a solution would also be in the interests of the United States.

There is hope that long-term peaceful trends may prevail, but it would be a mistake for the United States to ignore the possibility that the PRC might use force against Taiwan over the next decade. The possibility of U.S. intervention in the Taiwan Strait has been an important deterrent to war in the region since June 1950. Unfortunately, several current trends in U.S. foreign policy and national security policy might convince the PRC that Washington's intervention is becoming less and less likely.

First, there are widespread discussions of a substantial reduction of U.S. forces in the Asia-Pacific region. The administration is proposing to withdraw some American troops from South Korea and Japan and possibly to close Clark and Subic air and naval bases in the Philippines.[35] Beijing could take reductions of the U.S. military presence in Asia as indications that the United States would not likely commit major resources to preserve peace in the Taiwan Strait.

Second, the Bush administration considers the strategic importance of Beijing to be very great, as reflected in his decision not to punish the PRC unduly after the Tiananmen massacre. Beijing might interpret this reluctance to act against China as evidence that the United States would not intervene in the Taiwan Strait and even that the United States would resume normal relations with the PRC after a few months or at most a few years following the military defeat of Taiwan. For Chinese national interests, it is probably more important for Beijing to gain control of Taiwan under a reunited China than to have a few years of sour relations with Washington.

U.S. support for Taiwan is a major reason why the PRC has not attempted to use force in the Taiwan Strait. But there are other reasons as well: the lack of political incentive on the part of Beijing, the lack of readiness on the part of the People's Liberation Army for such a massive undertaking, the strength of Taiwan's own armed forces, and the need for Beijing to preserve its military assets to counter more serious threats from hostile neighbors.[36] Significantly, most of these incentives not to use

71

force are eroding at this time.

As Taiwan becomes more democratic and the majority of the Taiwanese population more openly discuss the merits of independence, for example, the political incentive for Beijing to use force against Taiwan may be growing. Political trends in the PRC are also toward a more hard-line approach to domestic and foreign problems. This may affect policy toward Taiwan. Certainly, Beijing has seen Taiwan, like Hong Kong, as a source of dangerous political ideas. The concern that Taiwan may be drifting toward independence and that Taiwan is undermining Communist party control on the mainland may help justify military intervention in the Taiwan Strait.

Analysts generally think that the PRC could take over Taiwan by military means if it is willing to pay a high enough price. That cost might diminish in the future as the People's Liberation Army improves its combined forces operations and amphibious operations. PRC strategists are discussing likely U.S. response to military action in the Taiwan Strait and Taiwan's defense capabilities. At what point the political gain of bringing Taiwan "back to the embrace of the Motherland" would be worth the military cost is a question that can be answered only in Beijing. But the question is being asked, and it should be kept in mind that the PRC has never ruled out the use of force.

Without question, Taiwan's own armed forces are getting stronger, especially in their acquisition of advanced military technology and the indigenous development and production of modern weapons. But it is enormously difficult for Taiwan to compete against China's large industrial potential and its massive production of ships, planes, and missiles. Unlike Israel, Taiwan's defense needs cannot be met by major purchases of advanced U.S. military equipment. The restraints imposed on U.S. arms sales by the August 17, 1982, communiqué and by other countries' reluctance to offend the PRC by selling arms to Taiwan require Taiwan to meet its defense needs mostly through domestic production. While marked progress in this area has occurred over the past few years, Taiwan's industrial and technological base is far smaller than that of the PRC. As the People's Liberation Army modernizes, it will be difficult for Taiwan to maintain, on its own, an adequate deterrent in the Taiwan Strait.

Finally, there is the restraint imposed on Beijing's use of force against Taiwan by the need to preserve the military to counter more immediate and serious threats to China's security. In the past these have come from the Soviet Union, Vietnam, and India. These threats, however, have diminished considerably over the past three years, largely because of Gorbachev's peace initiatives and New Delhi's and Hanoi's policies of

72

reconciliation with Beijing. Although the long-term threats from those countries remain, much of the rationale to preserve the People's Liberation Army to counter these threats has been removed.

Many of Beijing's incentives not to use force against Taiwan have therefore weakened, while the incentives to use force have grown somewhat stronger. The one exception is the growing interaction across the Taiwan Strait, especially Taiwan's investments on the mainland and tourists from Taiwan. But this interaction is a two-edged sword from the PRC's point of view. On the one hand, Beijing sees the interaction as a symbol of the ROC's commitment to a united China. On the other hand, interaction across the Taiwan Strait has not resulted in a favorable perception of mainland China by the people of Taiwan. As democracy expands on Taiwan, this perception may have an impact on Taipei's policies.

These various incentives to use or not to use force against Taiwan are summarized in table 4–1.

In sum, the PRC threat to Taiwan may be increasing, not decreasing. The 1989 elections are part of a trend toward more self-reliance and self-confidence on Taiwan's part. While Taiwan is not necessarily evolving toward independence, the PRC will likely become much more concerned over developments on Taiwan as a result of the elections.

Since most of the constraints on the PRC's use of force in the Taiwan Strait are being reduced, it behooves the United States to ensure that its credibility on the Taiwan issue is not lost. This necessitates a continued program of advanced military sales to Taiwan and the maintenance of adequate U.S. forces in the region to intervene in the Taiwan Strait, if necessary.

TABLE 4–1

INCENTIVES FOR THE PEOPLE'S REPUBLIC OF CHINA TO USE
FORCE AGAINST TAIWAN

Factors Influencing Decision to Use Force	Trends
Likelihood of U.S. intervention	Still uncertain, possibly weaker
Interaction across Taiwan Strait	Increasing
Possibility of Taiwan's independence	Slightly higher
Moderates vs. hard-liners in Beijing	Hard-liners in ascendancy
PLA strength vs. Taiwan's armed forces	PLA getting stronger
Threats to China from Soviet Union, Vietnam, India	Getting lower

Conclusion

Taiwan is evolving toward a parliamentary democracy. The new system will probably be characterized by a meaningful separation of powers and an adequate opportunity for minority parties to exercise considerable influence over legislation and executive behavior. Given the entrenched strength of the KMT, the probability that the DPP or another opposition party will gain control of Taiwan appears small for the remainder of this century. Nonetheless, the emergence of the DPP and its promotion of self-determination for the people of Taiwan have introduced an uncertainty in Taiwan politics that makes the future difficult to predict.

As in the case of Taiwan's economic "miracle," the fundamental political changes under way on Taiwan generally serve U.S. political interests. Taiwan is rapidly becoming a democratic state; its observance of human rights is improving steadily. If the people of Taiwan can successfully adopt the rules of democratic behavior, Taiwan may succeed in its objective of becoming a political as well as an economic model for mainland China and other developing countries. This would benefit the people of Taiwan, help moderate policies on mainland China, and fit in well with broader U.S. interests and objectives in the Pacific region over the next decade.

It should be recognized, however, that a quiet political revolution is taking place on Taiwan. The Taiwanese are assuming control over their own destiny. They no longer accept tutelage from the KMT. They want the power of choice to reside within themselves. This evolution in political consciousness carries vast implications for the KMT, Taiwan, China, and the United States. The outcome of the evolution has not yet been determined, since the people of Taiwan are only gradually realizing that they now have the power to determine their own future at the ballot box.

At a minimum, the people on Taiwan will demand and receive a greater opportunity to debate the issues that confront them. These will include open discussion of the pros and cons of Taiwan's independence, reunification, or maintenance of the status quo in the Taiwan Strait.

Moreover, the KMT will lose more of its power. This will not necessarily be reflected in poll returns showing less than 60–65 percent support for the KMT, but more subtly in a gradual loss of KMT control over the educational system, the mass media, culture, and other nonpolitical aspects of society. The military and security forces will attempt to protect the mission of the KMT and the ROC in influencing developments on mainland China, but that mission may become less widely accepted by the masses. As a result, tensions may grow between the military and the general population, particularly if the military becomes isolated through lack of sufficient KMT political support.

In the eyes of those dedicated to the recovery of the mainland, these trends may threaten not only their individual power but also the KMT and the ROC mission on behalf of China—a mission that has entailed great personal sacrifices for most of this century. It is true that Chiang Ching-kuo introduced many of the reforms that have swept Taiwan over the past few years and that the KMT's own doctrine calls for the eventual establishment of a constitutional democracy. Further, the KMT strategy since the 1950s has been to build Taiwan into an economic and political bastion from which an eventual return to the mainland might be possible. But has Taiwan become a bastion for the recovery of China, or has Taiwan moved in an opposite direction, becoming more independent from China?

A consensus has not yet been reached on Taiwan over this crucial issue. It is clear, however, that few people on Taiwan want to reunify with mainland China as long as the mainland is governed by the Chinese Communist party. Independence is an ideal to many Taiwanese, much like recovery of the mainland is an ideal to many mainlanders. It may well be that the ideal of Taiwan's independence may enjoy greater public support in the future.

This is not to say, however, that the independence of Taiwan will become a political reality. Many practical obstacles to independence as a policy block the way. Not the least of these is a strong possibility of an attack by the PRC and at best a 50–50 chance that the United States would recognize an independent Taiwan or intervene on its behalf if the PRC did carry out its threat to use force to prevent independence. But if one were to ask under what circumstances a policy of Taiwan's independence might be most likely, it would be, first, increased international support, especially from the United States, and, second, the inability of the PRC to do anything about it militarily.

Increased international support could be accomplished by vastly improved relations between Taiwan and countries such as the United States. This might occur if Taiwan begins to play a larger economic role in world affairs, thereby strengthening relations between Taipei and other capitals. If this development occurred at the same time that these countries' relations with the PRC deteriorated severely, then the circumstances might foster international sympathy for Taiwan's status as a separate nation.

Increased international support for Taiwan could also come about if the PRC decided to use force against Taiwan without provocation. Under these circumstances, countries such as the United States would feel a moral responsibility to aid Taiwan. Increased military and political support might then lead to improved political relations with Taipei, especially if the PRC proved incapable of compelling Taiwan to surrender. If, however, Beijing firmly committed the PRC not to attack Taiwan, few foreign countries would have the incentive to support Taiwan's independence. The interests of the United States and other nations have always been tied to a peaceful resolution of the issue, not to an independent Taiwan.

The second condition, the inability of the PRC to conquer Taiwan by force, could be brought about either by the adequacy of Taiwan's self-defense or by a severe weakening of Beijing's ability to use force in the Taiwan Strait. Taiwan's self-defense could be ensured if Taipei acquired massive amounts of foreign military technology and purchased great quantities of advanced weapons. A nuclear deterrent on Taiwan's part would probably not be adequate, if only because of the superiority of the mainland's nuclear weapons and delivery systems. A weakening of Beijing's ability to act in the Taiwan Strait could occur if the PRC's economy failed, undermining military modernization, or if political turmoil in China made a military adventure against Taiwan impossible to carry out.

The PRC seems determined not to allow Taiwan to become independent, but the December 1989 elections suggest that the Taiwanese people could move in that direction. Thus, Beijing will likely see the elections as a call to monitor events on Taiwan much more closely in the future.

As for the Chinese goal of national reunification, the Tiananmen incident and the subsequent political crackdown in Beijing could not have come at a worse time. The people of Taiwan, who are now beginning to exercise democratic powers, are unlikely to support Taiwan's reunification, even under peaceful conditions, with a government on the mainland pursuing policies so at odds with Taiwan's life style and standard of living.

Indeed, from a historical perspective, the most significant casualty of Tiananmen Square may have been the possibility of Taiwan's early reunification with the mainland. Peaceful reunification is still possible, but it will probably require at least four conditions: an agreement by the KMT and the Chinese Communist party on the timing and specifics of reunification; a consensus among Taiwanese that their interests are best served by an association with mainland China; a return to economic, social, and political liberalization in the PRC; and a credible U.S. commitment to a peaceful resolution of the Taiwan issue. Only the last of these, the U.S. commitment, existed as of the early 1990s.

Appendixes

Elections in the Republic of China, 1951–1986

TABLE A–1

RESULTS OF THE SUPPLEMENTARY ELECTIONS FOR THE
NATIONAL ASSEMBLY, 1969–1986

	1969	1972–1973	1980	1986
Voting rate (%)	54.72	68.52	66.43	65.43
Seats elected	15	53	76	84
Seats won				
KMT	15 (100)	43 (81.1)	61(80.3)	68 (81.0)
YCP	0	0	0	0
CDSP	0	0	1 (1.3)	1 (1.2)
DPP[a]	0	0	0	11 (13.1)
Others	0	10 (18.9)	14 (18.4)	4 (4.8)

KMT = Kuomintang; YCP = Young China party; CDSP = China Democratic
Socialist party; DPP = Democratic Progressive party.
NOTE: Number in parenthesis shows percentage of seats won.
a. Certain members of the political opposition proclaimed the formation of the
Democratic Progressive party in September 1986, and DPP candidates ran for
elections in that year. The government did not officially recognize the DPP, how-
ever, until after the Civic Organization Law was passed in January 1989 and the
DPP formally registered with the Ministry of the Interior.
SOURCE: Wu Wen-cheng and Chen I-hsin, *Elections and Political Development in
Taiwan* (Taipei, Taiwan: Government Information Office, p. 31).

TABLE A-2
RESULTS OF THE SUPPLEMENTARY ELECTIONS FOR THE LEGISLATIVE YUAN, 1969–1986

	1969	1972–1973	1975	1980	1983	1986
Voting rate (%)	55.00	68.18	75.97	66.36	63.17	65.38
Seats elected	11	51	52	97	98	100
Seats won						
KMT	8 (72.7)	41 (80.4)	42 (80.8)	79 (81.4)	83 (84.7)	79 (79.0)
YCP	0	1 (2.0)	1 (1.9)	2 (2.1)	2 (2.0)	2 (2.0)
CDSP	0	0	0	0	1 (1.0)	1 (1.0)
DPP[a]	0	0	0	0	0	12 (12.0)
Others	3 (27.3)	9 (17.7)	9 (17.3)	16 (16.5)	12 (12.3)	6 (6.0)

KMT = Kuomintang; YCP = Young China party; CDSP = China Democratic Socialist party; DPP = Democratic Progressive party.
NOTE: Number in parenthesis shows percentage of seats won.
a. Certain members of the political opposition proclaimed the formation of the Democratic Progressive party in September 1986, and DPP candidates ran for elections in that year. The government did not officially recognize the DPP, however, until after the Civic Organization Law was passed in January 1989 and the DPP formally registered with the Ministry of the Interior.
SOURCE: Wu Wen-cheng and Chen I-hsin, *Elections and Political Development in Taiwan* (Taipei, Taiwan: Government Information Office, p. 31).

TABLE A-3
RESULTS OF THE POPULAR VOTE FOR COUNTY MAGISTRATES AND CITY MAYORS, 1951–1985

	1951	1954	1957	1960	1964	1968	1972	1977	1981	1985
Voting rate (%)	79.61	74.85	78.20	72.49	69.05	74.26	70.31	80.39	71.94	72.08
Seats elected	21	21	21	21	21	20	20	20	19	21
Seats won										
KMT	17 (81.0)	19 (90.5)	20 (95.2)	19 (90.5)	17 (81.0)	17 (85)	20 (100)	16 (80)	15 (79.0)	17 (81.0)
YCP	0	0	0	0	0	0	0	0	0	0
CDSP	0	0	0	0	1 (4.8)	0	0	0	0	0
Others	4 (19.1)	2 (9.5)	1 (4.8)	2 (9.5)	3 (14.3)	3 (15)	0	4 (20)	4 (21.1)	4 (19.1)

KMT = Kuomintang; YCP = Young China party; CDSP = China Democratic Socialist party; DPP = Democratic Progressive party.
NOTE: Number in parenthesis shows percentage of seats won.
SOURCE: Wu Wen-cheng and Chen I-hsin, *Elections and Political Development in Taiwan* (Taipei, Taiwan: Government Information Office, p. 31).

TABLE A–4

RESULTS OF THE POPULAR VOTE FOR THE TAIPEI MUNICIPAL COUNCIL, 1969–1985

	1969	1973	1977	1981	1985
Voting rate (%)	63.98	60.57	70.65	67.89	65.53
Seats elected	48	49	51	51	51
Seats won					
KMT	44 (91.7)	45 (91.8)	43 (84.3)	38 (74.5)	38 (74.5)
Others	4 (8.3)	4 (8.2)	8 (15.7)	13 (25.5)	13 (25.5)

KMT = Kuomintang

NOTE: Number in parenthesis shows percentage of seats won.

SOURCE: Wu Wen-cheng and Chen I-hsin, *Elections and Political Development in Taiwan* (Taipei, Taiwan: Government Information Office, p. 31).

TABLE A-5
RESULTS OF THE POPULAR VOTE FOR THE PROVINCIAL ASSEMBLY, 1957–1985

	1957	1960	1963	1968	1972	1977	1981	1985
Voting rate (%)	78.20	72.52	69.26	74.28	70.33	80.40	71.94	72.08
Seats elected	66	73	74	71	73	77	77	77
Seats won								
KMT	53 (80.3)	58 (79.5)	61 (80.4)	60 (84.5)	58 (79.5)	56 (72.7)	59 (76.6)	59 (76.6)
YCP	1 (1.5)	0	1 (1.4)	0	0	0	0	1 (1.3)
CDSP	0	0	0	0	0	0	0	0
Others	12 (18.2)	15 (20.6)	12 (16.2)	11 (15.5)	15 (20.6)	21 (27.3)	18 (23.4)	17 (22.1)

KMT = Kuomintang; YCP = Young China party; CDSP = China Democratic Socialist party; DPP = Democratic Progressive party.

NOTE: Number in parenthesis shows percentage of seats won.

SOURCE: Wu Wen-cheng and Chen I-hsin, *Elections and Political Development in Taiwan* (Taipei, Taiwan: Government Information Office, p. 31).

TABLE A–6
RESULTS OF THE POPULAR VOTE FOR THE KAOHSIUNG MUNICIPAL COUNCIL, 1981 AND 1985

	1981	1985
Voting rate (%)	76.75	75.68
Seats elected	42	42
Seats won		
KMT	32 (76.2)	32 (76.2)
Others	10 (23.8)	10 (23.8)

NOTE: Number in parenthesis shows percentage of seats won.
SOURCE: Wu Wen-cheng and Chen I-hsin, *Elections and Political Development in Taiwan* (Taipei, Taiwan: Government Information Office, p. 31).

APPENDIX B:

Evaluating the 1989 Elections in China (Taiwan)

Raymond D. Gastil

To understand the broader significance of the 1989 elections in the Republic of China (Taiwan), we must recall that the people of Taiwan have had little if any experience with those civil liberties and political rights that we take for granted in modern liberal democracies. After years of Japanese occupation, the post–World War II period saw the imposition of still another authoritarian regime, albeit Chinese. From the viewpoint of many native Taiwanese, their island was occupied by an invading army in the late 1940s. After being pacified with the loss of many lives, it was treated as an occupied country under martial law until the late 1980s. During most of this forty-year period, criticizing this imposition was a grave and treasonable offense. All media were essentially a monopoly of the Nationalist party (KMT) and its political, juridical, and bureaucratic system, backed up by remarkably large and powerful security forces. (In giving this context, I realize there are good arguments for much of what the KMT did in the interest of nationalism and in response to the threat of the new Communist regime on the mainland, but this realization should not affect our judgment of the condition of civil and political liberties on the island during this period.)

Nationalist Taiwan was far from a completely repressed or controlled society during the early period of KMT rule. Some discussion was allowed among those accepting KMT premises, and leading roles within the party were privately, and occasionally publicly, contested by aspiring leaders, just as they are today in comparable authoritarian states. Yet those who disagreed with the system had nowhere to turn for assistance in the face of injustice. The executive, the judiciary, the local officials, the military, and police—even what organization existed in labor, business, and the professions—all were dominated by this same ruling mainland party. Those who opposed its rule often went to jail for their beliefs; a few even died for them. Many left the country to find new lives or to organize resistance movements overseas.

Gradually, the situation improved. In the 1970s, Taiwanese began to become more important within the KMT, and a few intrepid independents, loosely grouped as *tangwai*, began to take part in the political process with a modicum of success. A new wave of repression sent many leaders of this group to prison at the end of the 1970s. But the movement recouped. With the passing of the older generation of KMT leaders, repression eased. In 1986 the *tangwai* organized more formally as a political party, which, initially illegal, the government soon legalized. Martial law was abandoned in the next year, although some of its restrictions appeared to be retained in new forms. Whatever the legal niceties, under the new regime the opposition became more insistent, and demonstrations more frequent. For the first time, publications disagreeing with the government were allowed to appear regularly. Unions gained more independence. Opposition delegates fought hard for their views in parliament, even at times coming to blows. In those few local areas controlled by non-KMT leaders, local power was asserted at the expense of central control. Finally, in 1989 people could speak openly, if still with some care, of the possibility and desirability of Taiwan's becoming a state independent of China.

The Election

The 1989 election was more comprehensive than previous elections. Voters were asked to choose county magistrates or mayors, city councilmen, provincial assemblymen, and some members of the national legislature. (This election did not include members of the National Assembly, which elects the president.) For the first time party primaries were held before elections, and for the first time opposition parties participated legally in elections.

Election observers noted many problems with the process and questioned its political significance. The election could not transfer power on the national level. The legislature would continue to be dominated by persons elected in the late 1940s from the mainland and not subsequently required to stand for election. This circumstance, combined with other characteristics of the legislature's composition, as well as the need to build a more secure party base, led the main opposition party, the Democratic Progressive party (DPP), to concentrate on provincial and local positions.

The election and electioneering process was unduly restrictive. The two-week campaign was further limited by requirements for certain activities to take place only on a limited number of days within this period. Restrictions were placed on who could speak for a candidate. Certain

86

issues, primarily independence, could not legally be discussed by candidates or used to describe their positions. Many other petty legal constraints were noted. In the event, however, many campaign regulations were ignored or evaded.

At least as important as campaign restrictions were more general restrictions on the openness of the system. Some individuals still could not return to the country because of their past views. Imprisonment remained a threat, and a reality for some. The press was still mostly in the KMT camp, but not so predictably, and opposition papers and journals appeared regularly. The broadcast media were still totally controlled by the government and traditionally supported the positions of the government and ruling party. (This bias may have been moderated in the last days of the campaign.) Since campaign laws did not allow these media to be used by any party in the campaign, the built-in media advantage of the incumbents derived from the day-to-day reporting of political activities was magnified. In the bureaucracy, the judiciary, and even in the electoral commission, there was no significant change in KMT dominance.

The observers of the 1989 elections were also faced with a wide variety of accusations of dishonest or illegal election practices. Most of these accusations, however, remained without detailed documentation up to and through election day and were particularly difficult to quantify in terms of their likely effect on the outcome. It was widely claimed that there was a directed military vote targeted against particular candidates. It is no doubt true that people in the military voted KMT more than average citizens; yet the extent to which there was an organized and effective campaign to target this military vote on particular situations was unclear. Many charges of vote buying were made, and it is likely political machines on both sides did "buy votes." Since the KMT is more entrenched and wealthy, its candidates probably did the most buying. Yet again, the scale or nature of this buying was not clear; particularly unclear was whether money and presents were given supporters to ensure that they voted or were used in organized campaigns to change votes. (The latter is both more serious a malpractice and, because more difficult, less likely.)

The most significant procedural problem was the relative weakness of electoral commissions and the lack of opposition representation on them. Where the separation of the judiciary from government and party has not been established in the public mind, any major charges against the administration of the election or those taking part in the election—or demands for the nullification of particular results—could be brought before the civil courts only after the election. The reasons for the lack of opposition representation on the electoral commissions responsible for the administration of the election were in dispute. Evidently, the commissions had offered one or two seats to the DPP on its several levels. The commissions failed to respond to the not unreasonable request of the DPP for additional seats, however, and simply let the matter rest. It also appeared likely that the DPP believed that without a major role in the electoral commissions it would end up appearing by its presence to be legitimating commission decisions that it might wish to oppose. Since even if the commissions had accepted its requests, the DPP would still remain a small minority, it may also have been content not to take part. Whatever the reasons, this situation might have led to loss of public confidence as the electoral process unfolded.

The Significance of the Problems

In practice, this range of problems seemed to be much less significant than appeared at first sight. Of course, the election could not change the government at the national level, but the high turnout suggested that even this fact did not affect popular participation.

In spite of the short campaign, lack of access to the media, and other problems, the opposition got out its message—few citizens did not have a chance to learn what the differences between the candidates were (although these differences lay more in affiliation or character than in substantive issues). It is noteworthy that in India, a much less literate country whose broadcast media are government controlled and progovernment and whose elections are accompanied by widespread violence and other forms of interference with the process, the incumbent regime was massively rejected at the polls just a few days before the Taiwan election.

Election observers noted, and were told by members of the opposition, that there was relatively little fear in the election. Observation suggested that people had confidence in the mechanics of the election process itself, in spite of inadequate safeguards for the opposition.

Therefore, it was not surprising that the election saw a remarkably large turnout, about 75 percent, of the voters. The total vote for the KMT declined, while the opposition DPP improved its performance at every level. Opposition control of mayoralty or county magistrates rose from four to seven; of legislators, from fourteen to twenty-one. The KMT received only about 60 percent of the vote. Whatever the percentage, a recount has been called in one close election; this and other challenges may change the results in ways unlikely to favor the KMT.[1]

The Stage of Democratic Development and
Prospects for the Future

By the time of the election, Taiwan could be said to have a "dominant party" system similar to those found in Southeast Asia in Singapore, Malaysia, and Indonesia.[2] In these states, the media, or nearly all of them, are similarly controlled in one way or another by the government; the majority party has a stable majority, generally above 60 percent; and the opposition is kept hobbled in its position by a variety of restrictions on campaigning, organization, and freedom of expression. As in Taiwan, the maintenance of the imbalance in rights in the Southeast Asian states is justified by reference to a state mythology, varying with the particular historical experiences of each state—although their dominant parties have lacked a buffer against democracy of the dimensions provided the KMT by a legislature largely elected in the 1940s. In these states the dominant party's control of electoral outcomes in spite of the trappings of democracy has become so entrenched that it has been unaffected by the general world movement toward full democracy—indeed, in Malaysia the movement has been backward.

While the 1989 election in Taiwan does not fundamentally move the country above the level of these Southeast Asian states, it lays the basis for movement in the near future to much greater democracy. Several reasons suggest a substantial opportunity for forward movement. First, the stabilization of the dominant party's position in Taiwan's new, more competitive political environment has not yet occurred. Second, in spite of restrictions on the opposition in this election, opposition political leaders and publications were freer to criticize the system, and the general public was less fearful of following their lead in December 1989 than in the Southeast Asian states at this level of political development.

Another reason for optimism about democracy in Taiwan is the relative weakness of the political party structures that are necessary to ensure dominance. In this election the top-down effectiveness of the KMT in the bureaucracy, judiciary, and security services apparently did not carry over into competitive political campaigns. In this arena, KMT candidates often competed with one another. In several cases, if not nominated by their party, they ran as independents, sometimes effectively. Observers learned, and the results tended to confirm, that most people voted for individuals and that few "party votes" could be transferred from one candidate to another. This weakness could have been disastrous for the KMT if the opposition DPP had not been even more disunited and more dependent on highly personal machines or charisma. This suggest ed a lability of political allegiances that should make possible the creation of a more balanced political structure in the near future.

A final difference between Taiwan and the countries of Southeast Asia is its closer ties with the United States and Japan and thus with a more thoroughly democratic and Western world. Psychologically and economically, Taiwan is further from the third world and the authoritarian systems that still characterize most states there.

Obstacles to Continued Democratic Growth

KMT leaders now face the prospect that in a few years its built-in ability to control national politics will largely evaporate through death or retirement of the mainland representatives in the legislature and the assembly. They face this prospect with the political tide running against the KMT—in spite of the KMT's remarkable economic accomplishments and the obvious superiority of what it has achieved in all spheres, including political rights and civil liberties, to what has been achieved in the People's Republic. If it continues to allow at least the level of civil freedoms attained by late 1989 and the country goes through the inevitable economic and social ups and downs of all countries, the KMT will probably either be voted out of power within the next twenty years or the nature of its power will be fundamentally democratized (and thus comparable to that exercised by the Liberal Democratic party in Japan).

Several considerations diminish the likelihood that those in charge of the system will allow this to happen. First, while there have been many transitions to modern liberal democracy in recent years (no matter how unstable some of these might be), few of these developed in situations similar to Taiwan's. Most recent democratic transitions have followed immediately after the general moral and often economic collapse of repressive state structures—as in Argentina, Greece, Portugal, and now in portions of Eastern Europe. I do not sense that ruling structures in Taiwan have been undermined in a way at all comparable to these cases. In general, I imagine that KMT leaders see their accomplishments as many and their failures as few. They feel misunderstood, but not wrong. (Parallels closer to what democrats hope is happening in Taiwan exist in Spain, Brazil, and Pakistan, and it might be useful to look into whether the similarities of these cases can add to the analysis. But it is my judgment that even in these cases a general malaise in ruling circles made effective opposition to change nearly impossible.)

Another difficulty that some have in imagining that KMT leaders will allow nonviolent progress to full democracy is the lack of a national

90

background in democracy even as slim as that in the examples of democratic transformation just cited. While one should question the "cultural
conservatism" of those academics who believe that Chinese culture lacks
a basis for establishing a modern liberal democracy, the absence of experience with democracy makes both its establishment more difficult and
its destruction easier.[3] The opposition's tendency to resort to violence to
make its points, most recently during and after the balloting in Taiwan
and other areas in this election,[4] may eventually offer a cultural opening
for renewed repression. In the Sinic cultural area, however, Japan has
had a democracy more or less successfully imposed on it by an occupy-
ing army, and the success of this experiment has not been lost on the
Taiwanese.

If the old guard of the Nationalist party, supported by the security
services and the bureaucracy, do not step in to stop or reverse democratization, such restraint will likely be due to the rise of ever more western-
ized leaders within the KMT. Such leaders see Taiwan as a full partici-
pant in a world civilization in which modern liberal democracy is the
only accepted form of government. The 1989 election saw the further rise
of such leaders within the KMT, and it is evident that all parties, and
most sections of society, increasingly look to world models for their defi-
nition of acceptable behavior in many areas of life.

If this democratization of attitudes and values within the KMT
occurs, then in the next few years Taiwan will achieve full democracy
either through the attainment of a multiparty system allowing for alterna-
tion among the parties in power or through a mixed party system in which
public party factions serve much the same functions as parties; and the
general liberalization and rationalization of the other branches of government and society ensure a system that is neither repressive nor unrespon-
sive to the wishes of its citizens as expressed through the ballot box and
the countless other means available to citizens in a modern society.

On the Role of Outside Observers

In remarking on the current status of democracy in Taiwan after the 1989
elections, and on my expectations for the future, I wish to distance myself
from those who would demand before or after an election that officials
take one or another action that might strengthen democracy in the country. An observer may appropriately point out that certain actions would
be well or poorly received by the international community or that he per-
sonally believes it would be in the interest of the society, or even of the
ruling party or government, to take or refrain from taking particular

actions. But I do not feel that the outsider has a moral right to make demands, in part because he is unlikely to know enough to estimate whether his suggestions for speeding up or arresting change would be helpful to the society.

I do believe that the people of Taiwan deserve to live in a free society like any other people and that such a society can be achieved within an evolving Chinese and Taiwanese tradition. But the pace and exact nature of achieving this goal are neither my business nor my expertise—they are the long-term task of Taiwan's people. The purpose of the foregoing discussion is, in part, to point out that no one involved in the process of promoting Taiwan's democratization should minimize the difficulty of the job and the time it may take to achieve and stabilize modern democracy.

Electoral Institutions in Taiwan's Political Devolution

James A. Robinson

The electoral institutions, especially political parties and the Central Election Commission, that conducted the 1989 campaigns and elections illustrate Taiwan's continuing and still incomplete passage from authoritarian to representative government. This election to fill "supplementary" seats in the Legislative Yuan, to select members of the Taiwan Provincial Assembly and Taipei and Kaohsiung City Councils, and to choose county magistrates adheres to the pattern of political development that has been unfolding for forty years. This pattern is characterized by the government's and the ruling party's gradual devolution of power, wealth, enlightenment, skill, and other values *from* the émigré elite that occupied the island after the Japanese occupation *to* the rest of the population, now largely Taiwanese born since 1949. Such a devolution contrasts with the revolutions in Eastern Europe in the late 1980s when nonelites demanded and obtained increasing participation in political decisions from reluctant rulers.

The notable deviant case, so to speak, in the European saga is Gorbachev's introduction of gradual political and economic reforms. "Top-down," as distinguished from "bottom-up," reform is consistent with the political philosophies of both Lenin and Sun Yat-sen. Indeed, the KMT, as the party-in-government, very much resembles the Leninist model of the relationship between the Communist party and the government. A leading member of the Democratic Progressive party (DPP) said that when he enrolled in a Big Ten university many years ago to study for a doctorate in political science, he took a course on Soviet politics. As his professor outlined the Communist party in the Soviet Union, the student from Taiwan thought he was describing the KMT.

Taiwan's devolutionary process has been under way for much longer than Gorbachev's. Taiwan's now seems irreversible, perhaps even institutionalized. Gorbachev's may or may not be irreversible, but it is far from institutionalized and may even yet be replaced by more traditional revolutionary practices such as marked the Warsaw Pact countries in 1989.

Taiwan's electoral institutions in 1989 exhibited several important features of the strategy of political devolution. Some were new; others were a continuation of former practices.

Among the new elements was the greater openness of political discussion, whether on television, in the newspapers, in campaign speeches, or in conversation. As a result of replacing martial law, legalizing opposition parties, and removing limits on the number and size of newspapers, the context of campaigning noticeably changed. People who would not talk politics with this visitor in 1986 would in 1989. People would volunteer their intention to vote DPP. Even mid-level KMT officials would disagree with party actions. Little wonder that some DPP candidates dared to endorse independence despite the National Security Law. It remains to be seen whether and to what extent the government will prosecute their acts as sedition.

Another new feature was the introduction of party primaries by both the KMT and the DPP. The KMT's reform had the effect, presumably unintended, of increasing the number of second-generation mainlanders as candidates at the expense of Taiwanese candidates. While the mainlanders were largely successful in their campaigns, the primaries are subject to party appraisal for their expense and for alleged divisiveness. Soon after the election, the DPP announced its primary for the selection of a presidential candidate for the 1990 National Assembly convocation.

Continuing practices that stand out include the role of the Central Election Commission (CEC) in the conduct of both campaigning and balloting. The laws and regulations governing the CEC were revised three times in the 1980s, and most likely will be modified again before parliamentary elections in 1992. The CEC's rules reflect assumptions in Sun's ideas of "tutelary democracy" and of the governing elite's management of the transition to democratic practices. The campaigns, for example, are to be confined to fifteen days. While I have found no published rationale for this limitation, the justification one hears most often is that too many people should not be encouraged to devote too much time to campaigning. The explanation strikes one as grudging: "OK, but don't overdo it." In fairness, I acknowledge hearing references to parliamentary systems whose campaigns are significantly briefer than America's seemingly endless campaigns. In any case, the fifteen-day limit was breached earlier in 1989 than in 1986, and the CEC would surprise no one by modifying it.

Still another example of the CEC's campaign management, as distinguished from technical administration of balloting, is its sponsorship of rallies in the last week before the election. The commission arranges sites, provides audio equipment and lighting, names a presiding officer, keeps time, and regulates the selection and order of speeches. While I heard no criticism of the frequency or convenience (both times and places) of rallies, I did encounter chafing at limitations on who can speak. Students and persons from outside the district are ineligible for reasons not altogether clear but apparently intended to contain the extent of conflict.

The commission also publishes a gazette or election bulletin for each district. This multicolored newspaper includes candidates' pictures and information about place of birth (thus identifying mainlanders and Taiwanese) and other personal information. Brief statements of positions on issues are provided, but the commission edits these and in 1989 excised references to independence or secession.

The election law sets qualifications for office, including educational requirements. These are consistent with the Chinese tradition that emphasizes the relation between learning and governing. They are also consonant with themes such as tutelary democracy.

The administration of the CEC is part of the Ministry of the Interior. Its offices are next door to the ministry's. Its staff greatly expands during preparations for elections and then contracts afterward, returning to other duties in the Interior Department. Interior has few of the police functions, as in some polities, and its administration of elections resembles the role of secretaries of state in the American union. Still, perceptions that it is as neutral as comparable offices in, say Cook County, Illinois, linger.

Both the appearance and the fact of the CEC's neutrality will doubtless be improved as a genuine second party emerges. So far, Taiwan may be said to have a one-and-a-half-party, rather than a two-party, system. Nowhere is this more evident than in the administration of the election laws. Until now, the DPP has lacked enough active members to staff voting places as clerks or observers. Nor has it been offered places on committees created under the election law. Government officials have followed the European practice of admitting opponents to the administration of elections in proportion to their showing in the previous election. Hence, representatives of the inconsequential China Youth party have taken a few places that ought to go to the DPP, although in truth, the DPP did not respond to offers to recommend members for some election posts. This, I take it, stemmed less from lack of numbers or interest than from doubts about the legitimacy of election administration or from concern about endorsing election administration by even marginal participation. The appearance of the DPP chairman at the Central Election headquarters during ballot tabulation, however, indicated the DPP's increasing legitimacy and its increasing recognition of the legitimacy of CEC operations.

95

Taiwan's political devolution has been slow and measured for forty years. The pace of change accelerated between 1986 and 1989, largely exhausting the capital of reform accumulated and released by the administration of the late President Chiang Ching-kuo. A round of new developments is beginning under the leadership of President Lee Teng-hui. While the shape and form of succeeding changes are yet to be revealed, they will surely affect electoral institutions and practices. If the trend toward "democratization" is irreversible, the timing and introduction of new practices remain unclear. What is clear is that the period of tutelage is ending and an era of interparty competition *and* collaboration is beginning.

Notes

1. There has been a great deal of theoretical discussion over how to describe Taiwan's political system. Perhaps the best description is a "multiparty, but single-party dominant, representative government."

2. Japan gained control of Taiwan in 1895 as a result of its defeat of China in the 1894–1895 Sino-Japanese War. Prior to then, Taiwan was a loosely controlled province under the Ming and Qing dynasties.

3. The term "Taiwanese," which is used extensively in this book, refers to descendants of Chinese families who immigrated to Taiwan before the 1945 resumption of control by the Republic of China. Most Taiwanese are originally from Fujian Province or Guangdong Province. Because of the geographical isolation of Taiwan from mainland China and fifty years as a colony of Japan, Taiwanese have evolved an identity somewhat distinct from the mainland Chinese, or "mainlanders." About 2 million mainlanders fled to Taiwan in 1949–1950 following the collapse of the Nationalist cause on mainland China.

4. Troops under General Chen Yi, the appointed governor of Taiwan, severely oppressed the Taiwanese. When troops mistreated a Taiwanese woman on February 28, 1947, an ensuing riot sparked a rebellion throughout the island. Chen's troops reportedly killed up to 20,000 Taiwanese, mostly local elites and intellectuals. The February 28 Incident subsequently became a celebrated rallying point among Taiwanese nationalists seeking independence from the KMT and mainland China.

5. According to scholar Tien Hung-mao, an estimated 10,000 cases involving civilians were decided in military trials between 1950 and 1986. See Tien Hung-mao, "Taiwan in 1986: Reforms under Adversity," in John S. Major and Anthony J. Kane, eds., *China Briefing, 1987* (Boulder, Colo.: Westview Press, 1987), p. 137.

6. For an overview of the development of Taiwan's democracy through its elections, see John F. Copper and George P. Chen, *Taiwan's Elections: Political Development and Democratization in the Republic of China* (Baltimore: University of Maryland School of Law, Occasional Papers/Reprints Series in Contemporary Asian Studies, No. 5, 1984).

7. See appendix A for tables detailing these elections.

8. According to Chapter III of the ROC Constitution, the National Assembly has the functions of electing the president and vice president, recalling the president and vice president, amending the Constitution, and voting on proposed amendments to the Constitution submitted by the Legislative Yuan by way of referendum. Chapter VI of the Constitution specifies that the Legislative Yuan is the highest legislative organ of the state. It has the power to decide by resolution upon statutory or budgetary bills or

bills concerning martial law, amnesty, declaration of war, conclusion of peace or treaties, and other important affairs of the state. Chapter IX of the Constitution states that the Control Yuan shall have the power of review of the actions of public functionaries and of impeachment of these functionaries if they are found guilty of violation of law or neglect of duty.

9. The Chungli Incident of November 1977 was a violent clash between police and angry voters protesting against alleged irregularities in vote counting in the town. A district police station was burned, and several casualties were reported. See Tien Hung-mao, *The Great Transition: Political and Social Change in the Republic of China* (Stanford, Calif.: Hoover Institution Press, 1989), pp. 95–98.

10. Several victorious KMT had not been backed by the party but were elected because of their popularity with local constituencies.

11. An examination of the 1983 elections can be found in the testimony of Martin L. Lasater in U.S. Congress, House of Representatives, Committee on Foreign Affairs, Subcommittee on Asian and Pacific Affairs, *Political Developments in Taiwan* (Washington, D.C.: GPO, 1985), pp. 63–107.

12. A summary of this important election can be found in Martin L. Lasater, ed., *Democracy in China, Part Two: Taipei Style*, lecture no. 106 (Washington, D.C.: Heritage Foundation).

13. Article 4 states: "The territory of the Republic of China according to its existing national boundaries shall not be altered except by resolution of the National Assembly."

14. A cost of living index was later added, raising the value of the pension to NT $4.5 million ($167,000).

15. Penghu is the Pescadores Islands, and Kinmen is Quemoy.

16. There are three television stations on Taiwan, all of them controlled by the KMT or central government. The most influential radio station on the island is also owned and controlled by the KMT.

17. *Free China Journal*, June 5, 1989, p. 1.

18. Ibid., June 29, 1989, p. 5.

19. Lee Huan was replaced as premier by Hau Pei-tsun in May 1990.

20. The sixteen counties are Changhua, Chiayi, Hsinchu, Hualien, Ilan, Kaohsiung, Miaoli, Nantou, Penghu, Pingtung, Taichung, Tainan, Taipei, Taitung, Taoyuan, Yunlin. The five cities are Chiayi, Hsinchu, Keelung, Taichung, and Tainan.

21. Of the 724 candidates, 103 were women. Of the candidates 105 were second-generation mainlanders.

22. The maximum campaign expenditures equaled the total population of the constituency in a given district, divided by the number of public officials to be elected in the district, times the "basic amount." The "basic amount" was based on the categories of public officials, the duration of the campaign, the program of campaign activities, the size of constituencies, the communications circumstances, the candidates' overhead costs, and the price index of daily life necessities.

23. KMT officials explained this low voter turnout by noting that only about half the KMT members are active in party affairs.

24. The following is taken from "Platform of the Kuomintang of China," *Getting to Know the KMT Series*, no. 10 (Taipei, Taiwan: China Cultural Services, 1989), and other material distributed by the KMT to the AEI election observer delegation in December 1989.

25. The following is taken from *DPP: Democratic Progressive Party* (Taipei, Taiwan: DPP, 1989) and other material distributed by the DPP to the AEI delegation in December 1989.

26. It was difficult to determine the exact number of DPP candidates, because some DPP ran as independents or withdrew from the party just before the elections.

27. *China Post*, December 6, 1989, p. 16; *China Post*, December 9, 1989, p. 11.

28. Ibid., December 5, 1989, p. 16.

29. Ibid., December 4, 1989, p. 1.

30. Some evidence of this thrust emerged during the weeks prior to March 21, 1990, when Lee Teng-hui was elected president and Li Yuan-zu was elected vice-president by the National Assembly.

31. *Free China Journal*, December 25, 1989, p. 2.

32. See "Statement of the U.S. Congressional Observer Delegation," distributed at a press conference in Taipei, Taiwan, December 3, 1989.

33. For an extensive discussion of this policy, see Martin L. Lasater, *Policy in Evolution: The U.S. Role in China's Reunification* (Boulder, Colo.: Westview Press, 1989).

34. Mark Pratt, the U.S. State Department official in charge of Taiwan affairs during much of the Reagan administration, said in October 1985: "It is clearly U.S. official policy that Taiwan's future is not a matter of concern for the U.S., whose only interest is that any resolution of the Taiwan issue be arrived at peacefully. . . . [U.S. policy] is to emphasize the importance of peaceful means and not the end result." See Mark Pratt, "The Future of Taiwan" (Paper presented at the Conference on Major Current Issues in East Asia, St. John's University, Jamaica, New York, October 24, 1985).

35. An authoritative discussion of this can be found in *A Strategic Framework for the Asian Pacific Rim: Looking toward the 21st Century* (Washington, D.C.: Department of Defense, May 1990).

36. For a discussion of the incentives and disincentives for the PRC to use force against Taiwan, see Martin L. Lasater, *Taiwan: Facing Mounting Threats* (Washington, D.C.: Heritage Foundation, 1987).

The difficult issue of how to retire senior parliamentarians elected on the mainland in 1947 was resolved in June 1990, when the ROC Council of Grand Justices ruled that the remaining 768 members of the National Assembly, Legislative Yuan, and Control Yuan representing mainland constituencies must retire by December 31, 1991. The decision affected 76 percent of the total membership of the three elected bodies. The retirements would leave 84 members of the National Assembly elected for six-year terms in the December 1986 Taiwan elections, 129 Legislative Yuan members elected to three-year terms in the December 1989 elections, and 31 Control Yuan members elected to six-year terms in January 1987. The KMT will provide severance pay of

99

approximately NT$3 million (US$111,000) for each of the retiring members. *Free China Journal*, June 2, 1990, p. 1; June 25, 1990, p. 1.

Notes to Appendix B

This appendix was produced by the interaction of three kinds of experiences: putting together the surveys of freedom referenced below over the period 1972–1989, participation in a number of election observation missions as part of this effort, and seven days spent in Taiwan observing the elections as part of the AEI observation mission.

1. *New York Times*, December 6, 1989. At this point I do not know how the actual percentage is calculated; percentages may vary considerably, depending among other things on whether members of the KMT that did not run as official KMT candidates are included in the totals.

2. For the level of democratic development, see Raymond D. Gastil, *Freedom in the World: Political Rights and Civil Liberties, 1988–1989* (New York: Freedom House, 1989), especially pp. 32–37, 70–73, 368–69, 402–3, 421–22, 454–55.

3. For a discussion of the prospects for modern democracy in Chinese societies, see Raymond D. Gastil, *Freedom in the World: Political Rights and Civil Liberties, 1983–1984* (Westport, Conn.: Greenwood Press, 1984), pp. 119–317. This section entitled "Supporting the Development of Democracy in China" covers both the mainland and Taiwan. It includes papers by a variety of Chinese area experts followed by extensive discussion. Much of this is concerned with prospects for democracy and political culture, especially Lucian Pye's paper "Democracy and Chinese Political Culture" and the subsequent discussion.

4. *China Post*, December 4, 1989.